Acknov

I want to pay tribute to my fam
help and support this book wo

First and foremost, to my husba__ ___ _est friend, Patrick Thomas Flynn, who listened over and over to passages with unwavering love and interest.

To my daughter, Maggie Flynn Farley, who encouraged me from day one, and who took time away from being a mother herself to read and re-read.

To my son, Sean Patrick Flynn, who told me how proud he was of me, and sang my praises to anyone who would listen.

To my son, Evan Thomas Flynn, who told me that my dream could come a reality, and who would find inspiring music to encourage me.

To my son-in-law, Dave Farley and my daughter-in-law, Melissa Yoffee Flynn for their love, support and encouragement.

To my mother-in-law Suzanne Marvin Flynn, who handed me four diaries and allowed me to create this story, and who has always supported me as a mother and a friend.

To my dear niece Alissa and her husband Gary Karton for all of their love and encouragement.

To my talented and creative sisters Susan Hannen, Molly Gold and Amy Mullett for their love and kindness.

To my dear friend Sharon Dwyer, who took time out of her extremely busy life to help edit my book.

To the women in my business group of WIBIB who encouraged me from day one: Mari McNeil, Mary Barber, Marcia Brogan, Bonnie Roll, Lisa Brydges, Paula Damico, Amy Jo Lauber, Nancy Rizzo, Jamie Shaner and the entire group.

To The Harbor Girls, Marge Williams, Lois Barnum, Shelley Andrews and Cindy Goehle for their joy and laughter during those summer days.

I would like to express my sincere appreciation to Mary Kathleen Dougherty and her amazing staff at Roc-City Publishing for helping to bring my book to life.

And to Betty and Jimmie.

My heartfelt thanks to you all.

Dedication

To My Heart, Patrick

And my children, Maggie, Sean, Evan, Dave, Melissa

And my grandchildren, Avery and Emmett

And my dear mother-in-law Suzanne.

Introduction

On March 19, 1942 my husband's aunt boarded a train headed from Buffalo to Washington, D.C. She was twenty-one years old, and was driven by an overwhelming desire to help win the war. As it was in those days, her father had decided that sending her to college would have been a waste of money since she would undoubtedly marry. He did, however, subsidize secretarial classes to help her find a job until she could find a man to provide for her.

How very wrong he was.

Her career ended up spanning over 36 years and her service included secretary in the War Department at the Pentagon from 1942 to 1945; civilian duty in Japan during the U.S. Occupation; assignment in the Office of the Army Chief of Staff during the Korean War; secretary to the U.S. Representative, NATO Military Committee and Standing Group; secretary to the Air Deputy, Supreme Headquarters Allied Powers Europe; and secretary to two Administrators of the National Aeronautics and Space Administration.

She was the family's "matron aunt" and upon her death in 1998 my mother-in-law bequeathed her diaries to me dating from 1942 to 1945: her Cherry Blossom years.

This novel is based on her entries during those days. Names have been changed and some circumstances have been slightly altered, but the story is true. These people lived and loved and sacrificed. I believed their story is one that should be shared.

Within these pages every night,

Brief memories of the day I write;

A little word, a single line,

Is jotted in this book of mine –

Not mighty deeds, just common things,

The tasks and pleasures each day brings

And yet I hope that when I look

Over the pages of this book,

"Twill be (and, if so, I'm content)

The record of these years well spent.

Eloise Wood

A small pile of leather bound diaries belonging to my husband's Aunt Deborah sat in our attic among letters, photographs, match books and, scribbled on napkins from another era, bits and pieces of remembrances holding meaning only unto to her.

My mother-in-law knew that I journaled every day, and thought that I would find them interesting. Sadly, their importance fell way to the bottom of my, "When I have time to" list. Every once in a while I'd pick one up and leaf through it, reading of lazy summer afternoons, holidays with young annoying cousins, games of bridge, homework assignments, fashions, friends, politics, and boys, lots of boys.

Eventually I dusted them off and brought them down to my office where they languished for another four years, relegated to a desk drawer buried under report cards, bank statements and remind me notes.

One afternoon while cleaning out my office I decided to pile them on my nightstand, taking up space with a collection of other neglected reading material, half read books and tea stained magazines. Occasionally before I'd doze off I'd pick one up and read a few entries. Once in a while I'd catch some intriguing tidbit written in tight Catholic schoolgirl script, but I could never keep my eyes open long enough to follow the thread.

During a particularly long and dreadful Buffalo winter, I pulled out Aunt Deborah's diaries. I loved the way they held the scent of a library on a rainy afternoon. I dusted them off one more time, and decided to read them, this time cover to cover. I began with Thursday, January 1, 1942.

"Got in at 4 a.m. after a "grand evening out with friends ushering the New Year in, in style. Woke up around 11:30. Mother and Dad and I took Mrs. Miller out to dinner to the Peter Stuyvesant Room. I do so love their glass dance floor. We had a lovely time and a stimulating conversation on politics.

Mrs. Miller has extended a very cordial invitation to come and visit her for a few days. It'll give me the opportunity to see if I would like to live in Washington. What a thrilling thought! I'll talk it over with Mother and Dad of course, but I believe I will take her up on her offer."

A casual invitation over cocktails and politics, and Deborah's life was set in motion.

first met Deborah when I was twenty-two, and she was fifty-six, during the summer of 1978. She was sitting in my mother-in-law, Laura's flowery garden. It was a warm and welcoming afternoon with the clink of cocktails and female laughter rising above the giggles and squeals from the neighborhood kids swimming next door.

Jack and I had just come back from seeing, "Heaven Can Wait." Warren Beatty was still swirling around in my thoughts. We were young, and thin, and tan, and had recently become engaged a few weeks earlier. Aunt Deborah had just received the good news as we walked into the backyard. Laura and Deborah had their heads together sipping daiquiris and making wedding plans, all contingent on our approval, of course.

Jack had always been Deborah's favorite since the first time she laid eyes on him. He had gobs of dark hair and dark brown eyes. She called him her Botticelli Angel and had once exclaimed, "If I were to have had a child, Jack is exactly what he would have looked like."

Her hair had a purple tint to it in the sun, and was "done" in a fashion reminiscent of Nancy Reagan. She wore a stylish sweater, perhaps a little too youthful for her age, and white Capri pants. Everyone else was dabbing their brows, or fanning themselves with whatever was at hand, while Deborah remained untouched by the heat as though she had a way of controlling it. Her deep red nails were impeccably manicured and pedicured and she had a seasoned breathlessness to her voice. Waving her cigarette around in small circles she seemed important to me; impossible to ignore.

Over the years she would pop up in family photos, or old home movies, beautifully dressed, theatrically elegant, and always alone; no husband, no boyfriend, no one significant standing beside her. However, she would be sincerely laughing at something someone had said, or in deep conversation, listening intently, truly appearing to enjoy herself, no undercurrent of sadness.

Deborah would come to stay once a year with my mother-in-law. They were first cousins and as close as sisters. Whenever Deborah would enter a room you would expect an entourage to be following close at her heels. She simply filled a room with her presence. I didn't know what to make of this woman. She was like no one I had ever known, and I liked her immediately.

Laura had lived a safe, conventional, suburban life; marrying young, a soldier out of the army, having four children, with a dog and a cat and a built in pool in the back yard.

Deborah, on the other hand, lived in a condo in Washington, D.C., finishing up her formidable career at NASA, working for a man of great importance. This was how Laura described him.

As a young woman consumed with my own life at the time, I gave Deborah very little thought. As much as I liked her I also saw her as a relative who I was expected to engage in polite, obligatory conversation. I didn't really think of her as a real woman with an interesting history or hidden passions.

Since Deborah was a single older woman, I couldn't imagine she had ever had a boyfriend, or any kind of real love in her life. How very sad for her I recall thinking, poor Deborah living such a simple, passionless life.

When Jack and I were married, Laura encouraged us to honeymoon in Arlington, Virginia very near to where Deborah's condo was located in Crystal City. I thought at the time, how "Wizard of Oz-ish" that was, and how appropriate for Deborah. She could never live anywhere that had a mundane name.

Alexandria turned out to be a beautiful spot to spend our honeymoon, and I was grateful to Laura for suggesting it.

We were encouraged to connect with Deborah while we were there. We made plans to meet, at Deborah's suggestion, at the Mt. Vernon Inn Restaurant at 2:00 in the afternoon. She said the three of us would tour General Washington and Martha Washington's home and return to the restaurant for a late lunch.

As we walked the estate it was as though she were taking us on a tour through her own home; pointing out details and sharing stories with us from her past visits.

I found it touching when we came to the tomb of President Washington and Martha Washington. She described how General Washington had asked that his remains be moved, when the time came, to a new crypt, because the family vault was in need of repair and was improperly situated. I recall wondering at the time why Deborah referred to Washington as general instead of President.

She stood at the gates of their resting place with formality and quiet dignity, mentioning in a soft voice how very much in love the general and Martha had been. I wasn't surprised that she knew that, as Deborah was a historian with detailed knowledge of pretty much everything. She spoke so intimately about their relationship, then quickly composed herself and briskly suggested, "A lovely luncheon overlooking the Potomac, and that we must try their daiquiris."

Upon Deborah's death, twenty years later, my mother-in-law bequeathed to me a large packing box. Inside I found: Deborah's squirrel jacket with padded shoulders, her name embroidered inside, a rhinestone bracelet she received from her parents the Christmas of 1938, an autographed photo of Errol Flynn from the 1930's, a pair of earrings with a blue rhinestone center set in a ring of gold, her well-worn copy of Daphne Du Maurier's "Rebecca", a small leather bible given to her by her room-mate Jackie, and I came to realize, the greatest inheritance I have ever received from anyone: her journals dating from 1942 to 1945, along with a photo album and a silk blue box tied with faded purple ribbon full of letters – love letters from a Colonel Robert Munton.

BUFFALO, NEW YORK
Thursday, March 19, 1942

What a day! I did plenty of running around trying to get ready. I met mother for a late lunch downtown. We treated ourselves to an afternoon cocktail. I felt slightly wicked, but it was such fun celebrating my new adventure. Mother was being a darling trying to be stoic for my sake. She bought me a lovely box of stationery as a going away present. After lunch I had some essential shopping to do. I bought a new hat, stockings, panties, face cream, and two pairs of shoes.

Mrs. Miller wrote me a lovely letter. She hasn't found me a room yet, but said that I could stay at the YWCA until she can find me something nice.

I stopped in to see Mrs. Brown and I was so pleased that her sister was there so I could say goodbye to her too. She's been such a kind neighbor all these years, always offering me warm cookies out of the oven. I'll certainly miss that.

I had just finished my packing when Mother and Dad came in my bedroom with a gift for me, a lovely watch. I was thrilled! The girls from work took me to the Buffalo Athletic Club for dinner, a perfect send off. I played bridge with Mother and Dad and Mrs.

Brown after her sister left. It seems queer to be saying goodbye to everyone I've known all my life.

It isn't goodbye. I'll have to be stern with myself about that. I can't allow myself to get weepy for Mother and Dad's sake. I know how difficult this will be for them to see their only child off.

Friday, March 20, 1942

Thank God! It was a beautiful day, not balmy, but I'll take 48 degrees. It certainly beats the frigid days of February. Dad couldn't take me to the train because of work. I think it would have been too hard for him to say goodbye at the station anyway.

I took one last look around the living room I love so much while Mother waited in the taxi. I've spent the last twenty-one years of my life in this house, celebrating holidays, birthdays, entertaining friends and family with Mother and Dad. I had a rather queer feeling in the pit of my stomach, but I soldiered on. I was rather proud of myself for being so strong and not crying. I knew if I started it would open the floodgates for Mother and me both. We couldn't help but be a little teary when the train pulled out. She had given her handkerchief and I dabbed my eyes with it, not my nose. I wanted to keep her sweet scent with me.

It was a long trip, but such lovely scenery. A lot of draftees got on at Olean. They were hilarious, most of it forced perhaps. It was so pathetic when they got off at Cumberland Pennsylvania, lined up two by two. Mrs. Miller was at the station to meet me. It was grand to see a welcoming face. Two soldiers carried my bags off the train. I felt quite like the well-seasoned traveler.

It was so kind of Mrs. Miller to take me for a beer and a sandwich before helping me settle in at the YWCA, I was famished. I didn't allow all of the excitement to affect my appetite. Mother was worried about that. She knows how I get light headed if I don't eat on a regular schedule.

Thursday, March 26, 1942

My room is quite small, but clean and cheerful. I put Mother's hanky under my pillow, hope it doesn't make me more homesick. I wrote a long letter to Mother and Dad as soon as I got unpacked. The girl next door is moving back home. She painted an awful picture of Washington: shortage of men, long hours, and poor living conditions.

I decided to go get my hair done in Arlington to give myself a boost. I stopped by to see Mrs. Miller; she was so kind and invited me to share dinner with her. I would have been so homesick if she hadn't. I don't know what I would have done without her. She's been Mother's friend since they were children. It was sad that her husband died young. I was never told why. She was so in love with him she never married again. I'm terribly lonely in my room at night and was beginning to wonder, and have misgivings about working here.

I got acquainted with a girl who moved in next door after the crepe hanger girl left, thank goodness, and we had lunch together. I thought she was Chinese but she comes from Thailand. She's a doll and says she's a junior at Goucher College. She speaks perfect English. Her first name is Chauhan, but she said to call her Chummy. Her birthday is the same day as mine. I say that's definitely a sign that we will always remain good friends. I had breakfast and lunch with Chummy, and I was so dejected when she told me that she's going back to school in two weeks. We promised each other that we will stay in touch and write often. I guess girls come and go here rather quickly. I went to a news reel theatre this morning and there was a great deal of news about General MacArthur. He's certainly wonderful. We American's must have our heroes.

I wrote to Mother and Dad tonight and decided to go to the movies alone. "Dangerously They Live" was playing with John

Garfield. He's such a powerful actor. I've heard that he's rather short in real life. I don't believe I could ever date a man shorter than myself. I don't even like dating someone who is my own height. I like to look up to a man when I kiss him.

Tuesday, March 31, 1942

Mother and Dad feel much better about my getting along now since I've met another new friend. She's a perky girl who lives across the hall from me. We hit it off right from the start. Her name is Jackie and she went to the University of Wisconsin, she's a lot like Mrs. Brown's youngest daughter Betty. She's talkative and very enthusiastic, and she works at the Social Security Building. We'd like to get a place together, but she's already got an assigned room-mate on 20th Street and hasn't met her yet. Housing is pretty scarce and when space opens up you have jump on it. We sat up until 2:00 a.m. talking about our futures. This must be what it's like to go to college and live in a dorm.

Wednesday, April 1, 1942

War News:
India is to be granted dominion status by Britain in exchange for support in the Middle East battle ground. General Wainwright and his men on Bataan are successfully defending themselves against Jap assaults. R.A.P blasted decks at St. Nazaire.

Wonder of wonders! It's April Fool's Day in reverse. Jackie and I had supper together and then she suggested we take a taxi across town to see her new room. She very kindly offered to pay the fare. Mrs. Nelson, her land lady, was waiting for us. She reminds me a little of Tallulah Bankhead, but very nice.

After we took the nickel tour she told us that the other girl decided not to take the room, so I get to move in! I think she waited to offer the spot to me until she had a chance to look me over. It's a lovely big space with a large bay window across the front of the house. We get to see everything that's going on in Washington just by sipping our coffee at the little table and chairs that come with the room. We even have our own bathroom attached; such luxury. I hated scuffing down the hall with my bathrobe and slippers on at the "Y". The bathroom was all the way down at the end of the hall, and it was almost always occupied.

Jackie and I decided to go to see a double feature to celebrate our good fortune. There's quite a bit of snow and its bitter cold out, so we decided to spring for a taxi. I feel so grown up and independent.

I'm heading down to the Civil Service Recruiting Office tomorrow morning, they may have lost my requisition slip for my papers and I need to get a job soon.

Friday, April 3, 1942

War News:

General Wainwright and his Bataan defenders are withdrawing under huge Jap assaults. It's all so horrible. Well there's no doubt bombs will be falling on Washington before long.

I woke up this morning to the most wonderful news. I got a Job! I was assigned to Signal Corps. It is way out on 2nd and 3rd South West near the Potomac in a temporary building, but I don't care. I can't wait to tell Mother and Dad. Everything is falling into place so quickly. No reservations anymore. I'm where I'm supposed to be. I'm destined to live in Washington and work for the war effort.

I've been given my assignment - a secretary to a colonel. I haven't met him yet, but it all sounds so exciting. Jackie and I went to see "Foreign Correspondent" last night and it was thrilling. Everything here is thrilling!

Thursday, April 9, 1942

I'm so happy tonight my heart could burst. I love my work. I'm in the Army Communications & Equipment Coordination Branch. There are nine swell colonels, another girl, myself and a grand supervisor, Mrs. Perrault. All of our work is secret. How Hitler and the Japs would love the information I typed today. It's of the utmost importance that we never speak of the work that we do here or about anything at all that I transcribe.

My hours are terrific, 7:00 a.m. to 3:45 p.m. I get up at 5:15 a.m., but it's really easy. The city is so beautiful early in the morning. Everything smells so fresh and clean.

As soon as I came in this morning I was called into Colonel Baker's office to take dictation. He told me that they had advised Mrs. Perrault that all of the colonels were in complete agreement and want to keep me on permanently. I ended up working overtime for Colonel Baker and he offered to drive me home, (the long way around the park). He is quite flirtatious and I wonder what's up.

I bought some flowers for our room, just daisies, but they make everything seem so spring like. They certainly cheered up the room; those beige walls are so dreary. Mrs. Nelson said we could paint if we'd like to, but who has the time. I'm not even certain we could decide on a color. I'd love a soft blue, but Jackie said green. Maybe we could enlist some help from a few lonely soldiers at the USO.

I also bought a painting of the Washington Monument, with a beautiful yellow moon shining over the reflecting pool surrounded by dozens of cherry blossom trees. How utterly romantic it is. It gives me a thrill every time I look at it when I come home at night.

Friday, April 10, 1942

War News:

The news came today that the Battle of Bataan is over. The American-Filipino forces, after an epic struggle, had to give up from sheer exhaustion. A great many reached the fortress of Corregidor which is now being submitted to a savage Jap attack. This ended all organized opposition by the U.S. Army Forces Far East to the invading Japanese forces on Luzon in the Northern Philippines. The Island Bastion of Corregidor was the remaining obstacle to the 14th Japanese Imperial Army of Lieutenant General Masaharu Homma. The Japanese had to take Corregidor; as long as the island remained in our hands, they would be denied the use of Manila Bay.

It was a beautiful day today, 85 degrees out. We stayed outside all day long. The cherry blossoms are gorgeous. Jackie and I took a walk around the Tidal Basin at the end of the day and the cherry blossom trees were all lit up by the moon, just like our painting! They were not just lit up, but glowing with a magical aura around them. It made me think of home with my parents and Mrs. Baker sitting on our back porch.

How I remember when Mother would light candles and we

would listen to the radio. We'd play cards and Dad would argue over points. Mrs. Baker would have her knitting out. She's always knitting socks for soldiers. She said that's her part of the war effort. She even taught Mother how to knit, and I hear that I'm getting a yellow sweater for Christmas. I do hope it doesn't come out all lumpy, I would never want to hurt Mother's feeling by not wearing it.

Jackie and I couldn't believe how beautiful the Jefferson Memorial and Washington Monument were reflected in the water - such an inspiring sight. War is so very much upon us. All of the soldiers, sailors and their gals were out walking tonight. I was a little jealous watching them. You could truly feel that love was in the air. Love and war, two such separate ends of the spectrum.

When we got home there was a six page letter waiting for me from Mother. She sent me a new recipe for flourless chocolate cake, but we don't have kitchen privileges here yet. Jackie feels that Mrs. Nelson will cave at some point. I sat on my bed and read the rest of the letter with the window open. There was a beautiful breeze coming in and I had to be careful not to let Mother's pages drift around the room. I can't understand how I can stay up until midnight and then get up at 5:15. Privilege of youth I guess.

Saturday, April 11, 1942

I went out on my own today. I was so disappointed to see how awful the White House grounds looked. They are building an air raid shelter and it's ruining the landscape. The construction work all over D.C. is enough to make you cry. I find that I'm addicted to the cherry blossoms, they help to take my mind off of how everything else looks. I sat on the bank of the Potomac River and watched the sun go down. Then I went over to see the Lincoln Memorial again- I'll never get tired of it. Jackie went to the USO dance again. I would have liked to have gone, but going to a dance stag is something I've never done before and it would be hard to go the first time.

Grand surprise when I got back to our place. Chummy was sitting on our door step waiting for me. Thank goodness she hadn't been there long. She was in town to visit her aunt. We decided to go to the movies. "The Male Animal" was playing with Henry Fonda and Olivia de Havilland. I love her so, ever since I saw "Gone with the Wind". The way she played Melanie so sweetly was just perfection. I've seen GWTW five times and never get tired of it.

The theaters are making plenty of money now because people are seeking an escape from the reality of war. We took a taxi because it was raining. The driver dropped Chummy off at her aunt's first. I felt like Rosalind Russell sitting in the back of the taxi being driven through Washington. She always plays such strong women in her movies. The rain was relentless, but I loved it. I washed my hair and some undies when I got home and then peacefully slipped under the covers.

My pillows are so soft and Mother's quilt smells like her perfume. I hope her fragrance never goes away. I wish I had something that smelled like Dad, but I never did like his men's cologne. I'll have to write a note to myself to buy him some new cologne for Father's Day. I can never think of something to buy him.

I found myself listening to the radio and pretending that I was in love. I've never been truly in love before. Oh, I've had my childish flirtations back home, of course. But not that deep, even dark kind of love that swallows you up whole and never let's go. That's what I'm looking for. Sweet and simple isn't for me.

Monday, April 13, 1942

I took dictation from Colonel Munton today. He is so much fun and is terribly amusing. I think he looks a great deal like Errol Flynn, or maybe George Brent. Yes, much more like George Brent.

I came home to a fun surprise. Mrs. Nelson has two new kittens. They are adorable - an absolute picture. They are the star attraction in this house.

Mr. Thompson, the new tenant who is a photographer, took a lot of pictures of me in my room. He posed me himself; rather odd poses, smoking a cigarette, reading a magazine and turning on the radio. I'm really anxious to see the results. Then he took me out to dinner. He's very knowledgeable, knows just about everything there is to know about photography. And he's taken so many photographs of important people and places.

Friday, April 17, 1942

A black out of the district was scheduled for tonight. It gives me such a haunting feeling when it's so dark everywhere. I was relieved when the sailor that Jackie met the other night at the dance came around with another sailor friend. They took us to the Neptune Room and two other places in Maryland. I hate to admit it, but I can't remember the names of where we went. I'm afraid I had a bit too much to drink.

We had fun but I find young boys uninteresting. They tend to talk about themselves a great deal. How I wish I could meet someone older than myself, someone polished and debonair. Young boys fumble about with their obvious intentions. Intentions that ultimately go nowhere.

We stayed out until 3 a.m., and I got to bed at 3:30, and I had to get up at 5:00 a.m. I felt like a wooden Indian all day long at work. There was bad news on the political front: Pierre Laval has been made Premier of France. I know in my heart that this is going to be a very bad move for France.

War News:

The U.S. bombed Tokyo today and are they riled up. Its swell being on the offensive for once. Pierre Laval has full control of the French Government now, so it means full collaboration between France and Germany - a very sad state of affairs. Jackie and I went to the movies and saw "To the Shores of Tripoli," very stirring. It told all about the making of a United States Marine. You sure can't stop them!

Saturday, April 18, 1942

Here I am getting on in years. Twenty-two! I can't believe it. I had quite a birthday. Chummy gave me a manicure set and a bottle of cherry red nail polish. Jackie gave me a beautiful compact, she really shouldn't have. I know she doesn't have the money. She's such a good friend.

Mother and Dad called, Aunt Millie and Carol and Laura all sang happy birthday to me. I could tell Mother was tearful, but she quickly cheered up for me. Colonel Sheldon brought the entire office ice cream suckers, what a treat. He dictated to me while I ate mine. The colonel's seemed to be bowled over by the neckline on my blue dress. We all got out of work early and they took us girls to The Willard Room for cocktails. Then they took us for more cocktails and dinner to the 400 Club.

Tuesday, April 21, 1942

More fun at the office. Now that it's getting warmer out the colonels treat us to ice cream suckers every afternoon. I can't get over how kind the colonels are to us and the funny remarks they make; especially Colonel Munton. I dug out my Photoplay photograph of George Brent and I have it on my night stand. What a dream.

I met a very nice girl at dinner tonight. She's a daughter of a friend of Mrs. Nelson's. Her name is Sadie and she will be in Washington for a month. Her boss is here on business so she is here with him. Hotel expenses paid. Not bad at all! I got paid myself today $58.90. I wish all my expenses were being paid for.

I have to say, if my husband wanted to take his secretary away on a long trip to an exciting city I certainly would have a thing or two to say about it; especially with someone as young and attractive as Sadie. She has a darling short blonde hairdo. I don't believe I could ever be daring enough to cut my hair that short.

I'm having so much fun with the kittens. They sneak in our room when the doors open and jump up on our laps craving affection. We got to name them. I came up with the name Pixie because she's so tiny, and Jackie decided on the name Velvet because the bigger one is all black. They seem to know their names already too. When I come home from work I call out for Pixie and she comes right to me. Mother is so happy that we have kittens in the house. We could never have pets because Dad was allergic.

Friday, April 24, 1942

Sadie asked me out for dinner, and boy was I thrilled to go. She's staying at the Mayflower Hotel, what a dream to stay there. Her room is so elegant and yet, cozy. She even has a small terrace where you can sit out and have cocktails. She called room service and ordered two champagne cocktails. They brought them right up within minutes. We sat out on the terrace and could hear the mix of music drifting up from the room below and the soft hum of the city. I'm living a dream; I'm simply living a dream.

After dinner we saw one of the best suspense movies yet, "Saboteur." It certainly is timely; and so intriguing. Priscilla Lane was perfect in the role as the young innocent girl, I love the way she wore her hair. I wouldn't mind Robert Cummings kidnapping me anytime.

Sadie asked me if I'd like to come back to her room for another cocktail, but I thought I'd better not. I don't want to burn the candle at both ends.

I'm so glad I came home after the movie. My head hit the pillow and I was out like a light. I slept in until 10:15 and I could have slept some more, but I wanted to make the most of the day.

Saturday, April 25, 1942

War News:

Hitler made another raving speech today. He sees another year of war. He'll see that and more!

Jackie and I sat in the park today. It's so beautiful and spacious. Our Delaware Park at home in Buffalo seems so small in comparison. I could hear Glenn Miller's Moonlight Serenade drifting from someone's parked car. I can't believe they left their car running, what a waste of gas. The music was lovely though. It's all so romantic the songs they play now. I wish I could meet some smooth guy soon.

I went out tonight on a very impromptu date. Mr. Michael Kelly, one of the young sailors who came to see Jackie last week called me up. We had a long conversation over two bottles of Budweiser beer. He is a college graduate so, of course, I enjoyed talking to him. He was a little older than I had originally thought. He tried to kiss me goodnight, which spoiled everything. I did not give him any indication that I would accept his advances. Why must they all be like that? Mr. Kelly was not smooth at all, very rough around the edges, even for a college man.

I was so tired when I crawled into bed tonight. I said my prayers, which I haven't done in years. I need to make sure that I make more of an effort each night. Prayers are needed more than ever. To show how sincere I am I will even say a prayer for that Mr. Michael Kelly.

Friday, May 1, 1942

I went bicycle riding to Haines Point this morning. We got the entire day off because the colonels had a conference to go to. What a beautiful day, so warm with just a slight breeze in the air. This was a morning you write about. I rode for two hours. It was wonderful with all of the water all around, and the sweet scent of spring in the air. I felt just like a kid again.

Sadie is leaving Washington tonight. Her boss decided to head home earlier than they had expected. Jackie and I are going to miss her so. Washington is in her blood now and she said that she wants to come back to stay. I hope she does.

Mr. Thompson brought the photographs he took of me down to our room today. Jackie thinks he looks like Humphrey Bogart. Maybe a little bit. They turned out beautifully. He said I'm a good subject and that he'd like to take more pictures of me. I don't know?

Jackie and I went to see Carole Lombard's last movie, "To Be or Not to Be" with Jack Benny. It was devastating for Clark Gable when she died in that plane crash in January. She was so beautiful and they were very much in love, you could tell. Their love affair began when he was married to a much older woman. They had so much in common. She always seemed to be the kind of person anyone could walk up to and have a conversation with. She was real, not reel.

Tuesday, May 5, 1942

Jackie's friend Kate from Appleton, Wisconsin came in on the bus tonight. She's going to live with us. It might be a bit of a squeeze, but we'll make it work. We had a cake for her and a popcorn party in our room. I spent most of the evening talking to Manuel, whom Jackie met at a USO dance. He is foreign, tall, dark and handsome, and he's here training in the Army Air Corps on a scholarship. We talked all night about philosophy and he held the floor. He seems very well educated. I could never be truly attracted to someone who didn't have a college education. I need stimulating conversation.

Wednesday, May 6, 1942

War News:

The Island fortress of Corregidor has fallen to the Japs. 7000 prisoners have been taken. It's all so appalling. Colonel Baker said not to dwell on it or I will go crazy. It's just so hard not to.

I went out with Manuel tonight. Jackie didn't seem to mind. We went to a dance at the Soldiers, Sailors and Marines Club. Then we went to the Del Rio Night Club. He is such a good dancer and the fascinating accent of his is so pleasing. When you dance with a man in uniform it's entirely different. It's a feeling I can't even begin to describe. You feel as though you are in the arms of someone who will protect you always, and never let harm come to you in any way. It's intoxicating.

I got in at 4:00 a.m. and didn't even undress. The alarm seemed to go off one minute after I lay down. I managed pretty well at work considering I only had an hour and fifteen minutes of sleep.

Friday, May 8, 1942

Manuel and his friend Harry came over. A rather peculiar triangle has developed. Jackie likes Harry, Manuel likes Jackie and I like Manuel. What to do? We're all double dating tomorrow night. I'm not sure what to wear. Mother will have to send me a few more dresses from home.

I'm not sure where we will be going. I'm having such fun discovering Washington night life. Buffalo is grand of course, but it pales in comparison to Washington and all those wonderful men in uniform. They rather remind me of fire flies, lighting up the night and disappearing into their offices and barracks in the light of day.

Saturday, May 9, 1942

What a weekend! Manuel and I, and Jackie and Harry double dated. I decided on the new dress I got a couple of weeks ago. Why save it? It's a devastating color of cornflower blue. The neck line is a hair lower than Mother would approve.

We went to the Mayflower Cocktail Lounge and danced. Then we went to Balalaika's. We picked up some fun souvenir cards to remember the evening with. Manuel signed something Spanish on mine. After a "session" at the park we decided to stay up all night. We parked at Haines Point but couldn't sleep at all.

Monday, May 11, 1942

Manuel took me to the Premier of the Russian Ballet at the National Theatre. It was simply beautiful. I was excited over it naturally because it was the first ballet I had ever seen. The women were dressed so elegantly, right out of a movie. For a second I thought I saw Joan Crawford, but it was not to be. My imagination was getting the better of me. The music lifted me to a place I have never been. There was no war tonight, not in that theatre, only beauty.

When we got home reality reared its ugly head; there was a black out. It was very real, the sirens are terrifying. What a stark contrast to the ballet.

Jackie and Harry really seem to like each other. It looks like the real thing, but then when you're young it's hard to tell whether it will last. The kids are well suited, but Harry goes for the more glamorous life than Jackie does.

Friday, May 15, 1942

Manuel was over again tonight. He appears to like me a great deal. I'm not totally sure of my feelings as of yet. Gas rationing goes into effect today. Now we're really getting into war time sacrifices. I'm glad that I don't have a car. We won't be hearing any radios playing in the park again for a long time.

Manuel and I went for a walk. He has the most understanding heart of anyone I have ever known. His analysis of me is very good. I don't usually enjoy having someone tell me what I'm thinking, but he was right on target.

However, there could never be love on my part. There is a big difference between his culture and mine. From what I have read, women from his part of the world are more subservient than American women. Heaven knows I could never be subservient to anyone. That's just not in my nature.

I see no reason why we can't enjoy each other's company while he's in town though. And who knows how long he'll be able to stay here. That's the problem with dating a soldier. Here today, gone tomorrow.

Monday, May 18, 1942

I am working hard at the office. There is a perceptible increase in the work now that we are really swinging into war. I do admire Col. Munton; he's so much finer than any man I have ever known.

He is an excellent officer and so attractive. I would rather take dictation from him than anyone else.

Manuel and I ate at Mickey's tonight. I love their burgers and ice cold draft beer. I had my purple sweater on tonight, and I could tell how much Manuel liked it. He kept snuggling up next to me. He then took me to see "Reap the Wild Wind" right after. When I got home I didn't ask Manuel in. I have so much correspondence to catch up on.

Tuesday, May 19, 1942

Mother sent my laundry box back; all my blouses were neatly ironed. She enclosed my favorite book of poetry, Edna St. Vincent Millay, and my cologne and more stationery. She is so good to me and she never forgets a thing.

Tonight was the end of good times for the four of us. Certainly we shall never forget these days we have spent together. I know I shan't. Manuel was very sad tonight. He is a very melancholy person anyway and tonight more so. He leaves for a training field in Illinois tomorrow at 1:50 p.m. I felt it was better to say goodbye to him tonight rather than say our farewells at the train station. I will miss him. I do hope he understands.

Sunday, May 24, 1942

Lovely day. I worked from 10:00 a.m. to 4:00 p.m. to accumulate some overtime. It was swell, it was just the other girl in the office, Nettie, Col. Baker and Col. Munton. The two men took me home and it sure was a riot of a ride. They are a scream. Col. Munton is too attractive. I shouldn't keep saying things like that.

Men in their forties seem to go for young girls more than any other age.

Jackie and I went to services tonight at the First Baptist Church. It seemed nice being in church, very restful and good for the soul. I should have said some prayers for my impure thoughts about Col. Munton, but I didn't.

Friday, May 29, 1942

Jackie came in tonight with sort of a queer look on her face and I pumped her until I got an explanation. She and Harry have decided to call it quits for a while until he gets a chance to go home and see his old girlfriend Janet. It seems that he has some doubts. Also, his parents are quite upset over the whole affair. Well, it was sort of a sudden love affair anyway, so I'm not really surprised at the turn it's taken.

Lucky Col. Sheldon is leaving for "the front." He is the enemy of all the other officers (just kidding). They all wish they could take his place. He drove me home tonight and while we sat in the car he showed me his passport picture and told me that he will be a general staff officer. He said he regrets he will be leaving before he can "really get to know me."

I went out and bought a collection of the world's greatest speeches and a bottle of Jade perfume which Col. Munton recommended. He says it slays him.

I was told that soon the government will be calling up boys eighteen and nineteen. That is a definite indication that the war is not going well. It's really awful and just a few people realize it.

Jackie and I asked Mrs. Nelson if we could cook up a real meal tonight in the kitchen. She was thrilled to have the night off. We made Spanish steak, fried tomatoes, cheese stuffed celery, rolls, fruit salad and an apple pie. It was such fun cooking together. I'm going to take Mrs. Miller a piece of pie tomorrow. I feel so bad that I haven't visited her lately. I have to make more of an effort to check in with her.

Monday, June 1, 1942

War News:

The largest bombing exploit in aerial history was accomplished by the British yesterday, 1000 planes bombed Cologne.

Another colonel who works down the hall came in to say goodbye to all of us today. He's also going to "the front." One by one they are all leaving. It's so strange to think that when they leave

they may never come back. It's not at all like someone leaving their position where you work at an office. You know that you might see them on the street, or bump into them at the grocery store. With this there is finality about it all. Goodbye could mean so much more.

The big military parade was all I anticipated it to be. The armed strength of the U.S. is very impressive and one cannot help but be proud of our young men. I watched their faces as they marched; so young and determined. They are securing our future and they are proud to do it.

The climax was about one hundred tanks rolling down Constitution Avenue with sirens screaming. My heart was so full with pride to be an American. Coming to Washington was my destiny and I am confident that I made the right choice in leaving home to come to the heart of our nation. Tonight I'm going to write to Manuel.

Thursday, June 4, 1942
The Saturn Club of Buffalo

War News:

The Japs bombed Dutch Harbor, Alaska, twice yesterday. They are getting closer, next there will be raids on our Pacific Coast.

I thought of my friend Ruth from home who is getting married today. The reception is being held at The Saturn Club. I

34

so adore their courtyard in the center of the club. It seemed like I was stepping back in time when I would have cocktails there with Mother and Dad. Ruth's parents have always been so generous inviting us to join them. They'll be heading off on their honeymoon on Sunday. How I hope that someday I shall do the same thing.

I had loads of dictation. Col. Munton is giving me a lot of work so I can pile up overtime. I wore the Jade perfume he suggested. I could tell that he was pleased that I followed his suggestion and bought a bottle.

Saturday, June 6, 1942

Miss Jones, from Statistics and Reference Division, and I went to a Garden Party at the British Embassy for War Relief. The embassy is gorgeous, quite beyond words. In the main reception room there is a beautiful blue mirror and crystal chandeliers which hang, illuminating the cream colored frescoed walls. I found myself standing right next to Lord and Lady Halifax. If only Mother and Dad could see me now!

I'm really looking forward to going home for several days. It'll be great to see some of my old friends and sleep in my childhood bed. Everything has changed for me over the last few months. I have truly been exposed to so many new and wonderful things, and of course, terrible and frightening events as well.

Sunday, June 7, 1942

I worked more overtime for Col. Munton. I'm having dinner with Mrs. Miller tonight; the colonel drove me home so I would have time to get ready and not have to rush. How thoughtful of him. He took me to Arlington Cemetery. He said he needed to clear his mind. He's such a wonderful man. We had a marvelous talk. We stopped at a drug store and had ice cream. He has a new big blue Buick, so impressive.

Harry and Jackie came over to Mrs. Miller's for dessert, gloriously happy. It appears that the old girlfriend is out of the picture and Jackie is in. I'm happy for her; I just hope that Harry is sincere.

Col. Munton told me yesterday he would call for me at Union Station when I get back to Washington. He certainly is more than generous. The idea of him waiting for me is rather exciting. I can't help but be flattered by his attention. I haven't heard him offer any other girl in the office a ride.

I really shouldn't over think Col. Munton's offer. That kind of thinking could only get a girl in trouble. He's merely being kind to a young girl from out of town. I'm certain that it's more of a fatherly gesture than anything else.

I hope the lilac bush in our back yard is in full bloom when I get home. I love the way the fragrance drifts up to my window at night. Mother told me that she planted the bush there for just that reason. She's always thinking of me. She's such a dear. She sets the perfect example of what a mother should be.

Monday, June 8, 1942

It was such a thrill walking in the front door and seeing Mother and Dad again. The train didn't get in until 5:30 a.m. so I took a taxi home. Home. It's so strange to me now. I know that this will always be such a special place for me, but I truly feel that Washington is my home now. I couldn't believe that Mother and Dad were actually up so early. I called them from the station just to let them know I was home safe and sound and on my way. I couldn't wait to get into bed and just sleep!

When I got up I heard Mrs. Brown downstairs talking to Mother. Dad had to go to work. He'd never take a day off. I could smell the coffee and the warm cookies from Mrs. Brown. I knew she'd make some for me. What a treat. I'm so spoiled here.

Mother and I went to the movies and saw, "This Above All" with Tyrone Power and Joan Fontaine. It was beautifully done.

Saturday, June 20, 1942

War News:

The news is all bad. The British have lost a Fort in Libya. This German General Rommel is an evil genius. The Russians are trying hard to hold Sevastopol. Its outer defenses have been pierced by the Nazis. All signs point to a long war, which in fact I have maintained since the beginning.

Mrs. Nelson and I went down to the Watergate Concert. They played the viola concerts of Tchaikovsky, superb! She was very appreciative. After the concert she took me out for a cocktail. I had a gin and tonic. It really hit the spot.

Jackie, Kate and I held a bull session in our room tonight; war, love, marriage, men, boys, home town vs. Washington. I've lived here such a short time and yet this seems so right to me. Buffalo seems so far away, in more ways than one.

I'm very worried about Jackie. What was she thinking? She quit her social security job to take a trip back to New York. They didn't want to give her the time off. So, she's 4F, in debt - how in the world will she get out of this?

Friday, June 26, 1942

Col. Graham has been promoted to a full colonel. He's one of the older colonels. He gave me the honor of pinning on his eagles this morning. Quite a thrill. Col. Munton says he expects a kiss from me when the great day comes for him. Got paid today and I bought Dad two stunning Palm Beach neck ties for a belated Father's Day gift. I listened to Tchaikovsky's 5th symphony tonight. It is wonderful to hear music like that every once in a while. It takes you to another place, a place of peace and beauty.

Monday, June 29, 1942

War News:

More bad war news. The situation in Egypt is perilous.

Very exciting news. Our office has been moved to the Pentagon Building, it's a sprawling mass of enormity - it really holds one spell bound. We are on the 4th floor. The air conditioning really works too. There is a separate cafeteria for officers holding the rank of Major and above. Col. Munton's desk is near me so there is the usual comedy all day.

Mother wants me to come home for the 4th of July. I'm going to try to get Saturday off.

Saturday, July 4, 1942

Grand to be home. Beautiful, warm sunny day. Great to be with the family. I buried myself in the New York Times while lounging in the back yard and suffered slight sunburn because of it. Being in the office so much has kept me from getting any color at all. It will be nice to go back to work with a sunny glow.

I showed my snapshot album to the family and they loved seeing all of the sights of Washington. I hated saying goodbye. I still feel a pull for home. Buffalo is such a kind and homey city.

The train back to Washington was a streamline. Union Station was a madhouse when we pulled in. The holiday crowds were returning and they piled six people into each cab. It was the only way they could take care of everyone. I'm glad I had the copy of "The New Republic

Magazine" that Col. Munton gave me for the trip. It's a wonderful news analysis magazine.

Friday, July 10, 1942

I wore my new peep toe shoes today. Feeling very stylish. It started to rain at 5:00 p.m. I stayed overtime so Col. Munton could take me home. He sure is sweet - if he were single my heart wouldn't last long.

I met a cute boy at the USO tonight, Tommy Powell. We got in a conversation about the war. He is a Southerner and voted for Willkie in the last election. He said that "The New Republican" was a Red magazine.

Saturday, July 11, 1942

Tommy called. He lives in a fraternity house on Massachusetts Ave. He asked me over to the house tonight so I thought, why not and I went. We danced so well together, he is a marvelous dancer and then we played table tennis. Everyone was having such a grand time. They have a tremendous collection of music to choose from. One of the boys played the piano too.

Tommy asked me if I'd like to take a walk to the Tidal Basin. How can I begin to explain how beautiful it is here during the summer? It's so alive, so much going on, so many new people to meet. It was such a romantic atmosphere, and my usual romantic heart gave in to some love making. I do so love kissing, but I am very cautious not to let anyone go any further than that. He is one of the cutest boys I've ever met. I'm too cynical about men to expect he will call again.

It felt so good to lie on my bed and let the summer breeze wash over me. So much is happening to me. Is this all a dream?

Wednesday, July 15, 1942

You never know what is around the next corner for you. This evening I had dinner with Colonel Michael T. Stanford, the Chief of

The Communication Coordination Branch and his brother-in-law who is a full colonel. We had two cocktails each, dinner, then went to the movies. Colonel Stanford went to West Point and knew Gen. MacArthur. He even calls him Doug. Did I feel swell walking on the street with such high ranking officers.

Tuesday, July 28, 1942

I received a long letter from Manuel. It was quite romantic, some parts I didn't read to Jackie. He says he may join the yanks as a volunteer after his work for the Persian Government is over. I admire that in him greatly.

I don't want to lead him on however. I wrote him back with the tone of a very good friend.

I took Mrs. Miller to the Watergate concert tonight. It was an all Gershwin program, such a lovely evening, warm and sultry. She has been so good to me. It felt nice to be able to do something for her for a change.

As much as I enjoyed being with Mrs. Miller and catching up, I have to admit, I would have much rather been with Tommy, or Col. Munton listening to that romantic and moving music.

Saturday, August 1, 1942

War News:

On July 27, the city of Rostov fell to the Germans. It is going to be such a long war. It's difficult to try to remain positive when all of this stares you in the face every day. Will the world ever be the same again? I think not. Colonel Sheldon concurs. He feels this will be a very long war and many young men will die. He said that casualties of war will keep pretty young girls, like me, from marrying.

His statement is something I have believed for a long time. Will I ever be married to someone as fine as Col. Munton and have a lovely home and children? This is a dream that I have always had. I want a life that I can share with the man I love; a man I can respect and can stand by through the years, a man I can build a long and happy life with. It's what I long for, but will it ever come true?

Mother says that you make your own happiness. She says that you can't wait around for it to drop at your doorstep. I'm certainly going to make my happiness.

Friday, August 8, 1942

The war is eight months old today. It just doesn't seem possible. I really broke down at work. The homesickness just overflowed and I was so nervous I couldn't do my work properly. I began to cry, and Col. Munton was so kind trying to comfort me. He's such a doll. I told him how awful it was to be away from home. He sympathized entirely and said if there was something he could do for me to please let him know.

When I got home from work Jackie and Kate had made supper for us and even had a candle and a linen table cloth set on our small table. They bought a bottle of red wine and Mrs. Nelson loaned us three of her wedding crystal wine glasses. I certainly needed this. These girls have been like sisters to me. I should realize that more often. We haven't been to the movies very much and I think we need a girl's night out. "You know what they say about all work and no play," Kate said.

Writing down my thoughts is such a help to me. How very different my life is now. I have always kept a diary. When I look back and read what I was thinking and feeling, even one short year ago, I don't even know myself. I was such a young naïve child.

Mother and Dad have always been wonderful, but they sheltered me from so much in life. Now that I live on my own and can make my own decisions, and come and go as I please, I find that I have blossomed in so many ways. I've also had to realize that the world can be a very frightening place. Thank goodness I have my friends.

A girl needs friends she can rely on. It's such fun when we sit up at night discussing the young men we have met, and if they might be "the one." I haven't met anyone who might fit that description yet. I'm in no hurry. Mother has always said to me that you are only young once. Youth is not a time to squander your happiness.

Gee! I just happened to think - Pearl Harbor was just nine months ago today. A lot has happened since that fateful Sunday.

Very sad news in our office today. Col. Rundy's son who was in training with the R.C.A.F. was killed yesterday in a flying accident. This news will certainly break him. His life was bound up in that boy.

Col. Rundy's office is on the third floor, he's good friends with Col. Munton. I can't even imagine such a loss. The office is very quiet today, so solemn.

Kate and I went to see "Across the Pacific," a rip roaring good movie. It was good to go out after work and lighten our spirits. We have to remember that the youth of America has to stay strong and remain optimistic. This war is being fought for our generation and the next.

Three soldiers were sitting behind us making funny comments. Good to see their sense of humor is intact.

Sunday, August 30, 1942

The Hot Shoppe

I have been so busy at work that I haven't taken time to write in my journal. I was very down for a long period, and who wants to write about being low.

Col. Munton asked me to come in today for some overtime. I never would say no to him. We worked from 10:15 a.m. until 3:13 p.m. After work he took me to the Hot Shoppe for burgers and shakes. We had a long talk about marriage, life etc. Funny conversation to have with your boss. He is very interesting to talk to, very attractive, he is a big tease and extremely charming.

Wednesday, September 16, 1942

War News:

The Nazis have pierced the outer defenses of Stalingrad. Stalin wants a second front and I agree. They earned it, what a fight they are putting up. Willkie is in Egypt now.

There is a big bond drive on at the office. I am going to sign up for 10% of my salary which will absolutely do away with my raise. However, it is the least anyone can do. Every time I think of those valiant Russians still holding Stalingrad I think how much we really have over here.

The English seem to be all upset over Willkie's call for a second front. Churchill says all second front speculation should be muzzled. The House of Commons brought Willkie's name into the discussion amid much laughter. I don't like the sound of all that. Willkie deserves our respect, he has earned it.

Monday, October 5, 1942

I've been down with a terrible cold for days. I finally feel myself. It felt so good to be back at work. After a long day I came home to find Manuel waiting for me in his living room. He was dressed in the American Army uniform but couldn't wear 2nd Lt.'s bars because he is a foreigner. I got dressed all in black and Manuel was charmed. We went dancing at the Casino Royal. I had three Brandy Alexanders. So good!

Tuesday, October 6, 1942

War News:

Mr. Willkie is now in China receiving an extraordinary welcome, and Stalingrad is in its 43rd day of siege and still holding out.

I took dictation from Colonel Munton today. He is really adorable. I like him an awful lot. He seems so light when we're together. Sometimes I sense there is something he wants to share with me, but can't find the words. Perhaps it's my imagination, or am I seeing something that's truly there?

I took a walk after work today. The air is so crisp and fall like. I love the scent of leaves crunching under your feet and the rustle of the trees when an October breeze rushes through their branches.

Manuel called while I was eating and told Mrs. Nelson he had an important engagement and couldn't see me tonight. That's odd.

Friday, October 9, 1942

Jackie and I were just on our way to the movies tonight when Manuel called. So Mrs. Nelson went to the movies with her while I waited in the living room for him. I doubt if I'll ever see him again after tonight. I told him I could never fall in love with him so he shouldn't make love to me all the time. I tried to explain everything the best way I knew how, but he seemed very hurt.

Corporal Jake O'Malley is a new boy at the house. He took Mr. Thompson's room. Seems Mrs. Nelson didn't take kindly to "models" coming in and out of his room all of the time. Mr. Thompson assured her that as a photographer this was his profession and he needed to use models for his job. She didn't see it that way. There was a bit of an argument as he explained that he didn't have anywhere else to go. Mrs. Nelson said that she was sorry, but she had young girls to consider, and she was certain that he would have no problem securing another room.

I was surprised that she allowed another man to take the room, but Jake is a soldier and she said that it was her duty to accommodate him. She considered it part of the war effort. Jake has a very honest face, and he's Irish. You can always trust the Irish.

I was feeling pretty low about breaking Manuel's heart and Jake asked me if I'd like to go to the movies. We went to see "Tales of Manhattan" with Charles Boyer and Rita Hayworth. Very well acted.

I'd like to live in Manhattan someday. I can see myself in a posh upscale apartment living with a man of substance and socially elite.

Jake was a true gentleman. He never once tried to hold my hand or put his arm around me in the theater.

It's wise of him to take things slow since we are living in the same house together. How awkward it would be if I had to rebuff him immediately and then we'd have to see each other every day. A slow and steady course is the way to go. He is very attractive, I have to admit.

Sunday, October 11, 1942

Uh...Oh. Here we go again. Jake is a nice boy and he appears to think a lot of me. I have the feeling he wants to get serious about me. I know I could never fall in love with him. I want to set him straight right off the bat, that I'm not interested in a romantic relationship with him. He has that look in his eye when he's with me. And he hums a little tune whenever I come in the living room. He does make me laugh, and during these difficult times having someone who can make you laugh is a true gift you don't want to throw away.

We did have fun today. Early this afternoon Jake took a picture of me with a gas mask and steel helmet on. I have no idea how the soldiers can wear these and still be able to see where they are going and what they are doing. And I find it very difficult to take a deep breath. I only had it on for a minute and I had to take it right off. It will be a good photo to send home to Mother and Dad; on second thought, I hope it doesn't frighten them.

I got a letter from Chummy today. She's doing well at school and hopes that she will be able to come for a visit soon. She said that she got a new hair style and can't wait for my opinion. She said that she tells all of her friends how stylish I am.

I do have to make sure I write to her straight away. I heard that in a movie the other night. I can't remember who said it, but when they said, "Oh yes, I'll make sure to do that straight away." I just loved it.

Have to wash some delicates tonight before I go to bed. I shouldn't have let it go for so long.

Tuesday, October 13, 1942

It's been raining for days. I never liked rain in October. Next Friday night the office is having a big party out at Col. Baker's home in Maryland. The only trouble is that the colonel's wives will be there. At any rate, we ought to have a swell time.

Jake and Jackie and I went to see "Wake Island" with Brian Donleavy. It was rather difficult to watch. It was a thrilling account, and heart wrenching one too, of the famous fourteen days when Wake held the Japs at bay.

Mother enclosed a box of cookies in my laundry and two pairs of stockings. Boy do I need those. As I go to bed it's still raining. I'm leaving the window open just a crack so I can fall asleep to the sound of it.

Tuesday, October 20, 1942

I have been in Washington for seven months today. It hardly seems possible. The time has whizzed by, faster than at any other time in my life. There was plenty of work today. Col. Munton is still the same adorable riot and therefore is a great morale booster.

My pink sweater seemed to have the office all agog. Col. Munton did some of his best flirting. What a guy.

Jake bought me a toy dog. It is so cute. We named it Burp because it has a squeaker in it that makes a burping sound. We can't stop laughing every time we squeeze its stomach. It has white and brown fur and one eye that's a little too far to the right. I know that if I'm at a low point I can just hold on to my cockeyed Burp and I will feel better. It's always so comforting to have something, or someone, to hold on to during your dark moments.

Mrs. Nelson has given us girls another chest and a desk, both of which we needed. We asked her if we could paint the table and chairs by the window, blue, because they are a dull red and all chipped. She thanked us and said she'd buy the paint.

I spent a lovely evening with Mrs. Miller chitchatting over hot chocolate and cookies. She couldn't believe it's been seven months already since I stepped off that train. I had no idea what I was letting myself in for. She told me how proud she was of me and how much I have accomplished in such a short time. She is such a dear woman. I guess it is true, I have accomplished quite a bit in rather a short time. There really is no time to lose. Our country is in for the fight of its life and each one of us has a job to do. There can be no room for whiners or complainers; we're in this together.

There is a part of me that wishes I were a man so I could be a real part of "this man's army." I had been thinking of joining the WAC's, but I'm sure I would immediately be sent away and I just got here. For now, I'm going to fight the fight right here in Washington.

I've been trying to think of what I should be for Halloween. I don't really have many options. I do hope I don't get called into work. We're having a party and I haven't been to a real party in such a long time. Mother sent a big box of cookies as her contribution; her famous vanilla cake cookies with chocolate frosting. She packaged them so perfectly, not one smooshed cookies in the box.

Thursday, October 29, 1942

D.C. GIRLS GETTING JITTERS BECAUSE OF PANTY SHORTAGE

WASHINGTON —(UP)— Government girls report a drastic shortage in panties in Washington and what there are have no elastic to speak of and are held up by buttons, which in course of time come off.

According to a United Press survey, department stores believe the shortage is bad for morale because it gives the girls a feeling of uncertainty.

Reportedly the secretaries grow panicky when the shortage is mentioned. They say "buttoned panties are very hard to keep up," putting the accent on the "very." The Office of Civilian Require-ments is hopeful that the situa-tion might improve by October. Almost 450,000 pounds of silk parachute cloth rejects were re-leased for civilian use in August and in October manufacturers will be alloted rayon in amounts equal to 85 per cent of the Nylon consumption during the first half of last year.

An official said: "... But as for elastic, that's still out. The girls will have to get along using but-tons."

A switchboard operator sum-med up the psychological effect of the panty shortage: "You feel kinda lost."

I need some new undies, but it's not so easy to find them here in Washington. The guys from my old office sent me this funny news clipping about it. I've asked Mother to send me some from The Sample Shop, they have the best assortment

47

of colors. Kate and I went shopping on Connecticut Avenue. We went to four stores, none of which had any panties. I received a letter from my dear girlfriend Marsha in Buffalo. I do feel that I have neglected some of my old acquaintances. She said that Buffalo is dead as far as males are concerned. What are young girls to do? A shortage of panties is one thing, but a shortage of men is completely unacceptable.

Jake persists in his liking of me. He invited me to his room for a beer, but Mrs. Nelson made sure that we kept the door ajar. She does look over us girls like a mother hen. I certainly understand, especially with the situation with Mr. Thompson, although he never actually suggested anything inappropriate to me.

Saturday, October 31 Halloween, 1942

There's a new girl in the office. Her name is Maureen and she's from New England. She's rather lovely. I hope this won't create any competition between us for the colonel's attention. Ha Ha - sort of. She does seem nice though. I also remember what it was like coming into town like a deer in headlights. I think I'll invite her to our Halloween party at the house tonight.

When I got home my box of laundry from mother was there waiting for me with the rest of my fall clothes and extra panties. She included a box of brownies which were scrumptious. I'm saving those for myself. My Halloween costume was a scream. I wore Jake's fatigues and looked a riot. Several of Mrs. Nelson's friends were there too. Jake thought I looked better in those huge fatigues than I do in my green dress. I don't know what he has against my green dress. Personally, I think it looks lovely.

Maureen was very grateful for the invitation to our party. She brought a bottle of wine and some cookies her mother had sent her. I feel badly worrying about her being so pretty. She's actually married and her husband is in the thick of it. She's terribly worried not being able to hear from him very often. The colonel's explained that the mail can be difficult at this point and for her not to worry.

Sunday, November 1, 1942

I'm dragging a little today because our party went to the wee small hours of the morning. Jake and I danced most of the night, then he gathered us all together and began telling ghost stories.

He told one about a young soldier who was so in love when he died in battle, his sweetheart could hear him whisper I love you thousands of miles away. What a chill it sent through me. He put his arm around me and gave me a tender squeeze and then kissed my cheek.

My favorite ghost story has always been, The Legend of Sleepy Hallow. When Ichabod Crane was being chased by the headless horseman carrying his head that was shot off in battle, I still find that it sends shivers down my spine.

Col. Munton showed up at our door this morning with a box of doughnuts in hand, Buick running, imploring me to work a few hours for him today. I couldn't refuse. At least I got to go to our party.

We ended up working for six and a half hours. I was rather cold so he put his coat over my shoulders. I was thrilled, those eagles and field artillery insignias. He was perfectly adorable all day. Understanding is his best quality. He knows people so well, the why and wherefore of their emotions etc. It is too bad there are so few of his kind in this world. I'll always remember him as one of the best!

Tuesday, November 3, 1942

A typical republican election day dawned and ran true to form. Thomas E. Dewey is our Governor of New York State. Gee! I bet Dad is strutting around with a self-satisfied expression.

Jake bought me six beautiful red roses today. So romantic! The house is all shining with cleanliness. Mrs. Nelson was home all day and scrubbed every inch with the aid of a colored woman.

She loves how the table and chairs turned out and said she would pay us if we would paint her kitchen set. We said we'd be happy to do it for free, and she was thrilled.

The republican's gained 43 seats in the House and 9 in the Senate besides all the gubernatorial victories. This election shows that the people are sick of politics and want more action in the conduct of the war.

I went to the drugstore to buy some new lipstick. I tried out several different shades, sultry to coquettish. While I was trying to make up my mind Jake came up behind me and surprised me with a kiss. I think he's very attractive. Jackie does too, and I respect her opinion. There's something fascinating about the Irish.

Friday, November 6, 1942

War News:

The second front is going fine. Our forces are rolling across North Africa and slight French resistance is being wiped out. This is a remarkable bit of strategy as Africa is the spring board for an invasion of Europe.

Maureen invited me to stay overnight. She was very excited because she received a letter from her husband. I can't imagine how difficult this must be for her, for all wives of war. She made an incredibly wonderful meal; antipasto, spaghetti and stuffed celery, preceded by scotch high balls. I helped her while she cooked in her small kitchen. We listened to the radio and I taught her how to do the jitterbug/lindy. I can't imagine why she didn't know how to do it. Then she tried to teach me how to rumba, but we had to stop because we were laughing too hard.

We dined by candlelight and talked until 1:00 a.m, all about love and our experiences. While we talked I discovered that I am terribly fond of Jake. I wish I wasn't always at odds with my feelings. Maureen and I both took turns taking baths, then we stretched out in bed sipping scotch and sodas. What luxury!

Tuesday, November 10, 1942

War News:
The headlines tonight "Vichy French cease all resistance in North Africa," Nazis rush troops toward Tunisia to block U.S. drive. Many Frenchmen have joined up with the allies. That is terrific.

Jake and I had dinner together. The girls gave us some privacy and went to the movies. He had a blue V-neck sweater on and smelled delicious. I made him spaghetti and meatballs and we shared a bottle of wine. I feel so comfortable with him. He said I made the best meatballs he's ever eaten. We put the radio on and danced to Bing Crosby. Bing Crosby has such a dreamy voice. A girl has to be careful when she's listening to him.

Jake's office, the air transport command, is moving to New York on January First, I sure will miss him. I wonder if this decentralization of command in Washington will affect the signal corps. He gave me a beautiful present, three beautiful handkerchiefs, showers not blowers.

Well, it came; what I've hoped never would. The Director of Transportation has asked all government agencies to ban all civilian travel between December 18 and January 10. I had such plans and so many fun parties to go to. I'm very disappointed. I dread telling Mother and Dad. This will be my first Christmas away from home.

Sunday, November 15, 1942

I worked seven hours for Col. Munton. Afterward he took me to dinner at the Hot Shoppe. We had a long talk, very serious. I'm not sure what has brought this about, but I like it. I told him that Maureen was teaching me how to Rumba and he said he was quite good at it himself, and he'd be happy to take me out dancing some time.

One of his remarks amazed and thrilled me. He said if he were of my generation he would marry me. That is quite a compliment coming from so fine and brilliant a man. He also said he was very fond of me and cared a great deal what happened to me in this world. He said this was a very dangerous period in my life and I should be very careful.

Tuesday, November 17, 1942

Tonight I had a lovely romantic evening with Col. Munton. He spent about an hour and a half with me before he called for his children at the movies. He's never really talked about his family, but he told me tonight that he has a fourteen year old daughter, and a ten year old son. His wife's name is Helen, who takes care of the children and their home beautifully. He didn't have to say anything else.

He asked me if I would wait for him at my room while he took his children home. I didn't hesitate in saying yes. I had no idea what to expect. This is such a strong and powerful man, he's making decisions about the war that will affect countries. He's chosen me to confide in. I dare not disappoint him.

We drove around the river. It was gorgeous and so quiet. We had such a good talk. He pulled over and parked the car. There was a beautiful full moon. He asked if he could kiss me and I said yes, of course. In all my life I have never received such a perfect kiss. It was different from any other. I shan't forget this evening ever.

Friday, November 20, 1942

Jake wasn't home when I got in. He hasn't taken me out in weeks and it makes me furious. Living in the same house he takes me for granted. I'm just not going to be here all the time when he gets home.

Jackie and I went out to dinner with Maureen. We were eating in the Hot Shoppe when in walked Jake, obviously glad to see me. He brought me some carnations on the way home. Jake thinks I'm going to spend Christmas Day with him, but I'm not.

Mrs. Miller called me tonight and asked me to spend the holiday with her. How very kind and generous of her to think of me.

I'll have to think of something nice to bring for her. She's always doing things for others. I think she tries to occupy her time having lost her husband at such a young age. Someday I'm really going to have to ask Mother what the story is. I wonder why she never dated again. I know deep love is everlasting, but does it really have to be forever lasting?

Saturday, November 21, 1942

Came home to find a note that Harry had called. He and Jackie had cooled their relationship and she said she didn't ever want to talk about it. After several phone calls Harry and I planned to meet at Mrs. Millers where I was going anyway tonight with Jackie. I have no idea what is going to occur. Jackie refused to go. In the midst of all the hub-bub, Manuel rang the doorbell and was I amazed to see him! Jake's door was open and he heard all of this. When I left he was asleep and I went in to his room and turned off the lights, and the radio, and kissed him good night.

Harry looks perfect in his ensign uniform. He talked Navy all evening. I wish Jackie would have come. Maybe they could have sorted things out. Life truly is too short. More now than ever. I do believe she loves him too. So many young handsome men coming and going, I feel so badly for the girls back in Buffalo and the shortage of men. My cup runeth over!

The Watergate Inn
Sunday, November 23, 1942

Breakfasted in the main dining room of the Mayflower Hotel with Harry and his roommate. Harry left town at 3:00 p.m. having never seen Jackie. I still don't know what happened to them.

Worked from 1:00 p.m. to 7:00 p.m. for Col. Munton. It made me feel good. He took me to dinner at the Watergate Inn, a charming place with good and expensive food and candlelight, hobby horses are their theme. I felt like Cinderella at the ball. I could tell that he wanted to hold my hand across the table as other couples were doing, but, I understood. Just being there with him was enough. He spent the entire evening with me before he caught the train for Roanoke.

When I got into bed I thought about every minute of our evening together. We had a marvelous talk in the same spot as last Tuesday. I could fall in love with Col. Munton without blinking an eyelash. He obviously adores me and he says he'll miss me a great deal when he finally goes away. I hope that day never comes.

Mother's last letter to me indicates she is taking the news about my not being home for Christmas very well. I know how difficult it must be for them not to have me there. It will be the first time in my entire life that I won't be spending Christmas with my parents. I'm relieved that they are taking it so well. So many families are spending Christmas without their children, their husbands, and their fathers. We all have to remain strong at heart and will. It is a sacrifice, yes, but a sacrifice that each and every one of us must make.

What to get Col. Munton for Christmas? I can't begin to imagine. What do you get for the man who has made such an impression on you? I want it to be something that every time he looks at it he will think of me. Yet it can't be too personal. I wish there was someone who I could talk to about this. I could use some good advice.

I'm going to ask Jackie if she would do my nails for me tonight. What I'd give for a professional manicure!

Tuesday, November 24, 1942

War News:

The war news is good everywhere for our side. Hitler is taking planes away from the Russian front to send to North Africa.

I did some shopping today. I bought Mother a nightie and Dad a sweater. I got perfume for my little cousin Laura and a traveling kit for Jake. I bought a new hat with a veil, a navy blue sweater, and a white tailored blouse for myself.

Sunday, November 29, 1942

War News:

The news is so good. The Russians are killing so many Nazis I don't see how Germany can keep it up. The war in North Africa is going fine with our forces closing in around Tunis and Bizerte. Nationwide gas rationing is in effect today and coffee rationing as well.

I worked for Col. Munton today from two to six o'clock. Then he took me to dinner at the Hot Shoppe. We had quite a long talk in front of the house. I am really having a nice romance, something I did not dream would happen. He calls me "darling" a lot. I sincerely believe all he says to me is the truth.

I wrapped Christmas presents for home and addressed cards. After I had gone to bed tonight Jake broke into my room. He said he couldn't stay mad at me (imagine) and that he was nuts about me etc. There is such a great passion in this Irishman. The way his eyes crinkle when he smiles at me, so disarming. The Irish are truly magical.

Wednesday, December 2, 1942

I worked for Col. Munton until about 8:30. Afterward he took me to dinner. On the way home I got one of the best surprises of my life. As his Christmas present to me, he is going to pay my Pullman fare round trip to Buffalo when I'm allowed to go home to celebrate Christmas. This is the kind of thing I thought only happened in books. I am so happy tonight I don't know what to do. Mother sent my fur coat and evening dress, slippers and bag etc. She said that I should be ready for a big night out on the town for the holidays. She's such a dear. She thinks of everything.

I received a lovely card from Chummy. She's doing very well and says how much she enjoys my letters. She said my new friendship is a great gift. My heart aches for her, as she confided in me that people have been jeering at her with unkind names. She was on the bus going to class the other day and a business man looked at her, and looked at the empty seat next to her, and said, "I'd rather stand than sit next to a Jap." She said she tried to explain that she is not from Japan, but he wouldn't listen and no one came to her defense.

Friday, December 4, 1942

Worked again for Col. Munton. We had a late dinner at the Union Station Restaurant. At last I feel as though I was contributing something to the war effort. He said that I was of such help and that he would have been way behind in his work without me. I know the "field artillery" jargon and that's what is important.

It is impossible to record here the perfection, warmth and loveliness of my relationship with Col. Munton, or rather, it is our relationship. Taking dictation now from Col. Munton is most disconcerting. In between official dictation he says the loveliest things to me, and those eyes! They mirror everything, and so do mine. I feel that we know each other so well, almost as if we were from another time, and had gone through all of this before. We're rather like Lady Hamilton and Lord Nelson.

Jake was all excited when I got home from work. His kid brother Harold was getting in tonight at 8:05, so we went down to meet him at the station. He's enthusiastic, slim, tall, physically not at all like his brother. He rather reminds me of Jimmy Stewart. Wouldn't it be awful if I fell for Harold? I don't think I could ever allow myself to like a boy named Harold, so I'm safe.

Jake is shorter than Harold, but more muscular. However, their personalities are very much the same. We went to the Neptune Room and I got so dreamy on red wine. Jake was adorable and so easy to love. We danced all night. Poor Harold was slumped at the table exhausted. We finally took pity on him and took him home. I'll make it up to him and make some breakfast for the boys in the morning.

Sunday, December 6, 1942

I was starved until I got a big breakfast at 1:20 p.m. I slept in very late. It seemed a luxury to have scrambled eggs, bacon, toast and coffee. How perfect to have a day of rest. I spent some time picking up my room, ironing and of all things, I washed Jake's hair, an experience which he seemed to enjoy thoroughly. Tonight I went to the movies with Kate and saw a darling movie, "Major and the Minor" with Ginger Rogers and Ray Milland. He's so handsome, and I do love a man in uniform.

Monday, December 7, 1942

War News:

We have been at war one year today. Casualties amount to 58 odd thousand including dead, wounded, missing and interned in neutral countries.

Col. Munton's children, Lily and Carl, played host and hostess to Maureen and I tonight when we dropped off some work at the Colonel's home. Mrs. Munton invited us in for a cocktail and the children entertained us while their mother was in the kitchen making dinner. We were invited to stay, but I thought it best to decline. Maureen seemed a bit annoyed at my speaking for both of us.

I made it up to her by suggesting we go out for some fun. Maureen and I had a hilarious meal at the Hot Shoppe which I enjoyed exceedingly. I have not confided in anyone about the colonel's and my relationship. It is ours alone. Later this evening Col. Munton picked me up and we had a lovely long drive along the Potomac River. I didn't get home until after 1:00 a.m.

Tuesday, December 8, 1942

I received notice that I will have both Christmas and New Year's Day off. Tonight I had a date with Col. Munton. He picked me up at 8:30 at 19th and North Streets. Tonight it is the strong hand of fate that intrigues me. I would never believe in a thousand years this wonderful thing could happen to me. For the first time I have had the exciting thrill of hearing a wonderful person say, "I love you." Somehow there seems to be nothing wrong in this situation; it is lovely, heartbreaking and memorable.

Wednesday, December 9, 1942

When I got home last night there was a note waiting for me from Jake. He enclosed a poem he wanted me to read about the thoughts and feelings of a soldier. It just got me.

Yes, a soldier's day is always filled with mem'ries of his yesterdays:

The lips he kissed, the hearts he thrilled; A hand held tight within his own,

Now loosed-but-firm for country lent, this by a soldier-this his lament.

What reason then for tears to shed? Gloomy-pondering o'er the past,

for fear he's lost the life he led, no more return to hold that hand or kiss

those lips to his up bent is this the soldier's poor lament

Why, battles fought in years before still oft are told by veterans old.

Of rifle crack and cannon's roar and friends he lost on battlefield.

As he returned-thou, too-content. Why then-oh, Soldier-thy lament?

Fear not, America is this home! Stand firm, and let no foe prevail.

It was thy birthplace; twill be they tomb.

Have faith-and with your loved ones pray to end this waste of

life long sent and end thou Soldier -thy lament.

I am almost sure that Jake loves me. I shall always love him in a way. Part of my heart will belong to him forever. Why, I don't know. I've tried to analyze the attraction. I know part of it is mother instinct, because Jake has no mother. I feel like taking care of him.

Thursday, December 10, 1942

I met Col. Munton at 15th and N Street. Oh, it was so good to crawl, exhausted into that big comfortable Buick. We dined at The Watergate Inn. I expressed surprise when he suggested it. I said, "Oh, you're so good." He said, "No I'm not, I just love you that's all." Tonight he pinned his Field Artillery pins on me, the one he's had on every maneuver.

When I got home Jake came up to my room looking to see if he could find his Christmas present. He was so funny looking under my bed and in my closet. He wanted me to play hot and cold with him, but I didn't want him to find it. I haven't even wrapped it yet. He is a doll, I don't know why I like him. He asked me to look in on him after he went to bed. I did, and he was sound asleep, looking so peaceful and adorable.

Who will I be kissing under the mistletoe this Christmas? My Christmas stocking seems to be brimming this season!

Sunday, December 13, 1942

I had breakfast with Jake this morning, scrambled eggs, bacon, fried potatoes, toast and coffee. Marvelous! I went over to see Mrs. Miller for a short time this afternoon. We had a lovely conversation about the trend of the times. She has such interesting insight. Part of me would like to get her opinion concerning my love life, but I'm quite certain she would be a bit shocked. It was a little funny when she told me to be very careful. She said that I could be taken advantage of if I don't watch out. She said this is a dangerous time for young woman, and that a uniform can be blinding.

Col. Munton picked me up at the Buckinghouse Bus Platform at 5:30. We dined at our favorite, The Watergate Inn. I love him so much and I believe him when he says he loves me.

Monday, December 14, 1942

It's so funny when I think of everyone in the office. They wouldn't dream in a million years of this high romance that is going on right under their very noses. It's sort of nice to have a secret love affair.

Jake came home late tonight, but we had quite a serious talk. He undoubtedly cares a great deal for me and says he would propose if it weren't for this war. I know we'd never be happy, but I don't think he can see that. He is so loveable.

Tuesday, December 15, 1942

I worked for Col. Munton until 9:00 p.m. We had a late dinner at Naylor's Seafood Restaurant, and then we drove around the Tidal Basin. Mere words in this diary are so inadequate. How much I love him and in how many ways are impossible to describe.

He is so fine, good and understanding. These words I won't forget, "The humility of love is its greatest security." How this love will turn out I don't know, but I will never forget Robert. I don't believe he will ever forget me.

Wednesday, December 16, 1942

I unpacked the box from Mother and Dad this morning. I felt one of the packages and knew it was a picture, so I opened it. It was a marvelous colored picture of Mother. I am thrilled with it.

Tonight after I came home from the office I opened another box that was stationery that bore the U.S. Army and insignia in gold, Robert knew that I wanted some to write home with. Along with it was a little silver heart necklace with "To My" on one side, and "Forget Me Not" on the other. 1942 was "our" year. There was a note, "For you my love, a simple token before Christmas." How very sweet of him to think of me.

Col. Munton is flying to Ft. Bragg tomorrow. I will miss him so. How perfect that he gave me two hearts for Christmas, one his and one mine. I do so wish there was someone I could share this with, someone who I could show my gifts to. He told me that I must not ever tell anyone. Of course I understand.

Saturday, December 18, 1942

Jake and I went Christmas shopping on Connecticut Avenue. I bought a Donald Duck toy for the funny present at the office party. We had such a good time in the toy department. He told me that his favorite Christmas present ever, was a toy fire truck. He said after the war that's what he wants to be, a fireman. I was rather surprised. I had thought he wanted to make the air force his career.

After shopping we went to the movies to see, "You Were Never Lovelier," with Fred Astaire and Rita Hayworth. I so love the way Rita talks in a kind of whispery way. Very seductive.

I found that I couldn't stop thinking about Jake's wanting to be a fireman. I wonder if he was serious. I thought he might have wanted to be an airline pilot at the very least. Firemen serve an important purpose, of course.

Sunday, December 19, 1942

Jackie, Kate and I had breakfast at the Mayflower Hotel, an expensive and most enjoyable luxury. We exchanged presents. I gave Jackie some Evening in Paris cologne, and Kate, a darling pair of clips with blue rhinestones. Jackie gave me a box of stationery with my name and address on it, which I love! And Kate gave me a beautiful pair of white gloves. I don't know where she got them, but they had my initials embroidered on the cuffs. How elegant they are. I'm saving them for Easter Sunday.

There was a big tree in the lobby covered in tinsel and beautiful ornaments. It was so fresh, it smelled like a forest.

Col. Munton took me over to Mrs. Miller's for her eggnog party. We had some time alone to talk. It was a lovely brisk day with plenty of snow. He spoke about how this period is like no other time in history. He said how old conventions need to be boxed up and put aside while we, as a country, navigate our way through these difficult and trying times. He said that there is no promise for tomorrow, and that today is a gift we cannot squander. I will never forget this day.

I have to be careful. I wore my hearts on a chain to the office and more than a few people asked me about it. It was quick thinking on my part. I told them that it was a gift from Mother and Dad to remind me how much they missed me. At least now I can feel comfortable wearing them. My heart will always be next to his heart.

Monday, December 21, 1942

I met Col. Munton at 11th and G Street. We dined at Olmstrad's Restaurant and had a delicious turkey dinner. Tonight marks a new experience in my rich and varied life, or so it seems. For the first time in my life I went to a man's hotel room. With anyone else in the world I would have taken a big chance, but not with this one. It is impossible to describe how serene and perfect this feeling of security is. There was no fear on my part, no hesitation. Large white flakes of snow drifted past our window. It was like out of a dream. This was no boy that I was sharing this experience with; this is the love of my life.

Taxied to Union Station and saw him off to Fort Bragg. It was so difficult saying good-bye to him, to my love. What a magical Christmas this is. My heart is so full. I feel like a heroine in novel. This is like no other time. I need to remember that.

Tuesday, December 22, 1942

 When I came in the door tonight no one was home. Only the radio was playing, "It had to be you." When I called out as I hung my coat up, I thought how odd it was that someone had left the radio playing. Then Jake stepped out from the living room with a broad grin on his face and swept his arm around me ushering me through the doorway. There was a fire going and the tree was lit, a bottle of wine was on the table and a darling little plate of bread, cheese and grapes. I sat down, not knowing what to expect. I could never have anticipated what was to happen next.

He fell to one knee and took my hand in his. His eyes were so intense and almost pleading. He didn't have a ring because he said that he had to get it from his sister in New York. Their mother had put it aside for him for when the time was right. He did however have another small box for me to open. You can imagine my surprise when I saw what it was. There in red velvet cushion was an Air Force heart with small beautiful blue sapphires, and they were real. He had it made just for me. It makes a girl feel glowy all over to know she is wanted so much.

I had to say no of course, because I know we'd never be happy. We're poles apart. I could tell his heart was broken. He did not relent. Jake thinks someday, after the war maybe, I'll change my mind and marry him. You can't blame him for hoping. All I can say is I never really lived until I came to this crazy town. What a Christmas this is turning out to be.

He insisted that I keep the heart. He said it was made just for me and he could never give it to anyone else.

Thursday, December 24, 1942

Had a riotous party at the office with mistletoe and eggnog. When I got home Jake had another gift for me, a lovely dresser set. He's really pushing it. Mrs. Nelson gave me a yellow hand knit sweater with matching socks. More eggnog was had by all. Mrs. Nelson's eggnog didn't have the kick that the eggnog had at our office.

When the girls came home we all sat around Mrs. Nelson's piano and sang Christmas songs. Silent night is always a killer for me, especially since I won't be home for Christmas this year. I really miss Mother and Dad. My being their only child I know how hard it must be on them. I rallied and insisted we sing Jingle Bells.

The tree was simply beautiful, all lit up with tinsel hung delicately on each branch. The room smelled so fragrant, like we were all standing in the middle of some great pine forest. Mrs. Nelson had on a lovely green velvet dress, which set off the silver in her hair beautifully. She looked like she should be featured on a Christmas card herself.

When I placed my head on my pillow tonight I said a prayer of thanks for so many wonderful gifts in my life.

Friday, December 25, Christmas 1942

I woke up to a winter scene etched on my window. Big white flakes of snow continue to fall and blanket this beautiful and grand city. The girls and I went to Mrs. Millers around 1:00. We had a quick cocktail together at our table in front of our window, and we were off. We took Mrs. Miller a bouquet of pink roses and heather. She greeted us at the door with more eggnog and hugs. She simply loved our gift.

We had a good turkey dinner, but it didn't hold a candle to Mother's. I didn't feel too badly at being away from home today, as I knew that Mrs. Miller would have been alone without us.

Mrs. Miller asked me to join her in her bedroom for a moment. Her bedroom wallpaper is covered in lilacs and she has such a divine dressing table. It's so much like the one I have at home. She pulled open the drawer and handed me a small box. Inside was a beautiful simple bracelet. A small crystal ball with a tiny seed inside attached to a silver chain. She said her mother had given it to her when she was twenty one, and since she didn't have a daughter, she wanted me to have it. There was also a little story folded up inside. It told of the power of faith through the Mustard Seed parable from the Bible:

Matthew 17:20

"He said to them, "Because of your little faith. For truly, I say to you, if you have faith like a grain of mustard seed, you will say to this mountain, 'Move from here to there,' and it will move, and nothing will be impossible for you."

What a lovely Christmas present. I do have mountains to move, and I do have faith.

Saturday, December 26, 1942

War News:
The papers are full of the assassination of Admiral Jean Darlan.

Monday, December 28, 1942

Jake has a bad cold so I took off this afternoon to take care of him. He says he's the proudest guy in the world. I put Vicks drops in his nose, made lunch for him, fed him soup and gave him aspirin. I also saw that he got his dinner. Mother always said, "Feed a cold, and starve a fever."

Maureen and I went to the movie to see Bette Davis in "Now Voyager." I was riveted from beginning to end. It was the story of a woman who was in love with a married man. They could never marry because of his obligations to his family. I was captivated by the Bette's characters last words. "Oh Jerry, don't let's ask for the moon, we have the stars." My heart was so full when we walked out of the theatre.

Jake felt much better when I got home. I sat with him for a while and brought him a cup of tea with hot lemon and a shot of Irish Whiskey. Mrs. Nelson provided the whiskey. He'll sleep tonight!

Tuesday, December 29, 1942

I looked in on Jake before I left for work. He was sleeping peacefully. I put another blanket over him and tiptoed out. I wanted to make sure that he as tucked in and warm. It's snowing very hard this morning. I hope we don't get a blizzard.

I worked for Col. Munton. There is nothing like working for the man you love. We had dinner at The Watergate Inn, marvelous shrimp Creole. I can hardly believe it. Here is a man who will always love me no matter where I go.

Thursday, December 31, New Year's Eve 1942

Col. Munton took me out for champagne cocktails after a day of furious work. He had dinner guests waiting at home and had to rush off.

Jake and I were all set to go out when suddenly the war intruded. A phone call ordered Jake to Balling Field for a test flight. At 11:15 he called me from Norfolk in a hurried and breathless voice to wish me a, "Happy New Year, darling." I have to admit, I was thrilled. He doesn't seem to be at all put off by my refusal to marry him. He seems very confident that I will change my mind, perhaps he's right.

Mrs. Nelson had some friends in for drinks. I joined the party but was in bed shortly before midnight. When I heard horns blowing and people wishing each other Happy New Year, I couldn't help but think that Robert was kissing his wife at the very moment.

January 1943

Saturday, January 2, 1943

Jake and I went to see "Gentleman Jim" The life of James Corbett the boxer. Errol Flynn was so dynamic in it. I've never seen him in anything where he wasn't perfection. Col. Munton got my train reservation both ways, as promised, for my Christmas present. Not sure how I'm going to explain this to Mother and Dad. Maybe I'll just say it's a gift for being a very good employee. It wouldn't be a lie.

Jake and I had breakfast together as usual. I spent a lot of time cleaning up my room this afternoon. Jake and I had dinner tonight, as well, at the Alda's Garden. He's been very solicitous to me ever since he proposed. I do hope he's not trying to change my mind, poor boy. I haven't been leading him on in any way. At least I don't believe I have. It's rather strange, it's as though he has a renewed spirit.

Monday, January 4, 1943

I worked for Col. Munton for a little while tonight. At frequent intervals he'll look at me in that way I'll never forget. Then I feel as if my heart were going to stop beating. We had dinner at the Watergate tonight. I do love having a place that is all ours. Butter rationing permits one pad of butter to a customer. That's a good way to keep a girl's figure slim.

We parked in our usual place. This is such a beautiful war romance. He loves me terribly, much more than I realize I guess. Imagine, two men love me, a corporal and a colonel.

Tuesday, January 5, 1943

Jake was already home when I came in. He made love to me for a while and I cried for the first time in my life about a boy. He has this beautiful Irish face, and he's so young and handsome. The way he looks at me with such utter love and trust. I cried because he

70

loves me so and I can't love him in the same way. He seemed to understand perfectly and was very gentle and sweet. I guess I'll remember that moment with him forever.

Wednesday, January 6, 1943

I worked for my own sweet darling until about 7:00 tonight. It is most difficult to get anything accomplished. We had dinner at Naylor's and I literally wallowed in a whole Maine lobster. He does spoil me so. We talked a great deal during the meal. I told him all about Jake and how I felt about him. He helped me analyze the whole situation. I hardly know my own mind sometimes. He explained to me all about what love really means, and how to look at it clearly.

When I got home Jake was waiting for me. He wanted to say goodbye because he's going on a trip with six generals. He, of course, could not even hint as to where he was going. He'd had his overcoat pressed and looked very snappy and neat. I know I'll miss him.

I caught a glimpse of the headline regarding Roosevelt's message to Congress, "Victory Maybe in 1944." There are new restrictions out on driving cars. No driving to restaurants or movies, bowling alleys, night clubs etc. At the end of the war we'll all be in excellent condition for sure from all our walking.

Friday, January 8, 1943

I met Col. Munton at 11th and G Street this time. We dined at Olmstead's Steak House. I was so hungry. I had a thick steak with mushrooms, absolutely delicious. Still only one pad of butter though. That's the way it is now in all of the restaurants.

We can't park anymore in our favorite spot around the Tidal Basin. The police are busy hauling people in for joy riding. We found a dark street and stayed until a little after eleven. Stolen Heaven are the words.

There was a telegram from Jake waiting for me on the table by the door when I got home. He said he'd be coming in at 1:30 a.m. and to try to wait up for him. I simply couldn't. I was curled up on the sofa and couldn't keep my eyes open. I was so exhausted.

Monday, January 11, 1943

Jake brought me some presents home, a lovely embroidered handkerchief with little blue flowers, and pearls from Lord & Taylor. I just love my presents. Jake is so good to me.

Maureen and I went out cocktailing tonight at the Carlton Hotel Bar. I had two daiquiris and felt fine. We decided to be plutocrats and took a taxi to the Olmsted's. I had turkey for $2.00, some fling for a war time budget. I got home early and ironed undies. Jake wasn't in too good a mood tonight, seemed tired.

I'm knitting some mittens for Jake, blue with a red strip. His hands always look so cold. I think I'll make him a matching scarf, and I could put some white tassels on the bottom, red, white and blue!

Wednesday, January 13, 1943

We are all excited and pleased as a peach. The Board has been reorganized as the Army Communications Board and have been put directly under General Charles, the Chief of Staff. We're at last out of the Signal Corps and where we belong.

I went over to Mrs. Miller's tonight for dinner. It was typically war time fare with one helping of everything for each person, sausages and fried apples and baking powder biscuits. She also had a nice bottle of white wine. I usually prefer a heavier cabernet at this time of year, but beggars can't be choosers.

Col. Munton called for me at Mrs. Miller's at 10 p.m. We sat parked in the car on the N. Glenn Road. He is so desperately in love with me that it makes me feel so unworthy of it sometimes. I know absolutely that no other man in my life will love me as completely, or as well.

I have to have faith that all of this will work out in the end for everyone. I'm taking life one day at a time. I have all the time in the world to think life over and make my decisions. It's like Scarlet O'Hara said, "After all, tomorrow is another day."

Friday, January 15, 1943

Col. Munton has selected me to do all of the stenographic work on air amphibian. I sat in on a conference this morning and took notes. He said I did very well. This is all so very exciting I can't believe it is truly happening to me.

Met Jake at 12th and P Avenue. He took me out to dinner at the Neptune Room, haven't been there in a while. Then we waited in line to see Bob Hope and Bing Crosby in "Road to Morocco." It had an impossible plot, but it was a scream from beginning to end. When we got home we sat in the living room with the lights out and talked for a while.

The snow was falling so silently, illuminated by the street lamps which gave us a small amount of light. Dear, dear Jake, his heart is so full. If only I had more time to think clearly. But I am thinking clearly. My heart will show me the way.

Saturday, January 16, 1943

I went home for my "Christmas in January." It was wonderful seeing Mother and Dad. Dad picked me up from the station and he asked me to tell him all about what I have been up to. I hope he didn't see the blush come to my face.

I had lunch with Cousin Carol, movies with Betty from next door, and sledding with a few of the kids down the street. I was a wreck when I got home. I had a splitting headache and the horrible windy bitter weather combined to make me fit for a grave. But oh, to come home and find the lovely red roses from my love. Two dozen! There was a card with one word, "Nelson." Lord Nelson and Lady Hamilton, what a charming game this is to play. After a long nap I came downstairs, Mother had a table top tree all set up with my gifts under it. We had a big Christmas dinner with all of the trimmings. Uncle George, Aunt Millie, Laura and Carol were there to welcome me home. Carol said she would like to come and visit me if I wouldn't mind. I felt a twinge of sadness for Laura, as she's too young for a trip to Washington right now.

We all played "society craps" and I won 97 cents. Jake called me, just to check in. How he ever got a hold of me is more that I can know.

"Society Craps" Rules to the Game

You need pennies or nickels, a deck of cards, a pair of dice, and a dish of some sort (for the "kitty"). Each player chooses a suit and receives all the cards of that suit. Lay out the cards in numerical order in two rows as, face up, but discarding the seven and the king:

2, 3, 4, 5, 6

8, 9, 10, 11 (jack), 12 (queen)

Each player receives a pile of pennies or nickels, 40 or 50 each is a good starting point, but everyone should have the same amount. Place the "kitty" in the middle of the table and everyone "sweetens" the pot by throwing one penny into it. Now each person takes turns rolling the dice. If they roll a number on  one of their cards, they flip that card over. If they roll a 7 or a number they've already flipped, they throw a coin in the pot. The first person to flip over all of their cards wins the "kitty"!!

If played in earnest, you would eventually want to be the last one left...with all the coins!! How rich you will be!

Sunday, January 24, 1943

Mother, Dad and Carol saw me off on the train. Mother was waving her hankie and looking stoic and darling. Dad was doing everything he could to remain unmoved, but he has never been one to hide his feelings well.

I quickly found my berth and began opening my suitcase to settle in. I suddenly had the sensation that someone was standing way too close to me for comfort. When I turned to give a grim look of disapproval, there stood my beloved Robert. This couldn't possibly be!

From that moment on I memorized every scent, every sight, and every sound of the evening on that train; although it was difficult to take in anything other than Robert standing there in his uniform.

Now I know the meaning of one night of perfect love. My darling gently took my arm and guided me through the narrow passage to the drawing room he had booked ahead of time for the two of us. He simply nodded to the porter, who followed behind us with our bags.

There were two dozen red roses waiting for me, a bottle of champagne with chilled gimlet glasses on a silver tray. He knew I would be famished. There was a bowl of fruit, cheese and crackers and a box of Belgium chocolate. It was the most intoxicating experience of my life. When we were finally alone, he swept me into his arms and kissed me and told me that he had been waiting and planning for this moment for so long.

We spent a loving and tender night together. I'm so glad I brought my lovely black nightie. No possession, just love. Oh I shall remember this forever! Mere words are futile to describe it.

We had breakfast in the dining car and I ordered a Bloody Mary, how decadent. Watching the scenery passing by gave me a sense of what my life might be like, beautiful images fleeting by. As preplanned, we separated quickly as we got off the train in Washington, and took separate taxis, how clandestine it all was. I went home and unpacked.

Jake was overjoyed to see me. He had another gift for me, a beige leather traveling case, all fitted with everything I would need.

I went into the office at noon, Robert wasn't there. I don't know how I will be able to get up and go to work every day and not want to take him in my arms. Oh what a secret.

Tuesday, January 26, 1943

War News:

Tonight at 10:00 an important news cast came on. President Roosevelt and Winston Churchill have been conferring in Casablanca and have laid down allied strategy for 1943. High officials of both counties were present. The whole allied world should thrill to this news.

Robert loves me so. How I hope I can be worthy of such love. Lord Nelson and Lady Hamilton could not rival our love, truly. Just think, I used to think this only happened in books and movies and now it's happening to us.

I find myself daydreaming at times. I need to be careful of that and stay focused. Too much is at stake.

Wednesday, January 27, 1943

Air-amphibian conference today. I took notes. It's very exciting. Now that the Board is under the Chief of Staff we have broad powers. Quite a set-up in fact. Being a part of all of this is such an honor.

Robert brought me home in a taxi tonight. In fact, each day so far this week. This love is so perfect it hurts, and is terrifying at times.

Jake took me to see "Casablanca", it was timely, thrilling and romantic. I was spellbound right through. I was so tired when we got home I went right to bed. I do wish I had been able to see this wonderful movie with Robert.

Saturday, January 30, 1943

Today is the 10th anniversary of Hitler's rise to power in the German Reich.

Jake and I braved the usual Saturday night crowds to see "Commander Strikes at Dawn." It was a very good picture of Norway invaded by Nazis. We walked home through the deep snow.

We should have taken a taxi, unfortunately, Jake can't afford one. When we got home we made a fire and warmed our feet in front of it, then I let Jake make love to me.

I don't really feel that I truly belong to anyone man right now. It really isn't fair to Jake I know, because I love Robert and I could never really love anyone else. At least, that's what I feel today. Who knows what will happen today or tomorrow. We have to live for right now.

Monday, February 1, 1943

I have been suffering lately from a urinary burning. Robert made an appointment for me with a doctor, a fine specialist in women's diseases. Wednesday he will know what is causing the affliction. We worked for about an hour tonight. We sat in the Pentagon parking lot and talked and loved so desperately. I cried terribly. It's the future I'm afraid of. The years are so long. Everything is like a blind alley, just a maze.

Wednesday, February 3, 1943

I took notes at the air amphibian meeting. It's going to require plenty of night work. I spent two and a half hours with Robert this evening. I am his dream, the one he's had for centuries. Here we are and we can't retreat now. The Lord above has his plans for us and we can't force any decision.

Oh, I called the doctor this morning and he assured me that everything was okay. The analysis was perfect. It is just a minor irritation and nothing to worry about.

My laundry box came with my sweaters done up beautifully. Mother enclosed a lovely bracelet and my perfume tray. It's always such fun opening my laundry box because I never know what added treats Mother will supply.

Monday, February 8, 1943

Beloved and I worked on air amphibian this evening. It requires a great deal of detailed work, but I do feel as though I am accomplishing something important.

Sometimes I feel so unworthy of Robert's great love for me. No one in history could have loved me more. He told me tonight that I was duty, honor, love, country, home and family to him. It is true that I will never be loved by any other man like this again in my life.

This is much worse than the single tab of butter. Shoe rationing started today! You are allowed three pairs of shoes per year and only one pair between now and June.

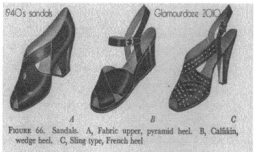

FIGURE 66. Sandals. A, Fabric upper, pyramid heel. B, Calfskin, wedge heel. C, Sling type, French heel

The Air amphibian conference in the Under Secretary of War's conference room. It was super, as nice as I expected. Taking notes is difficult. The officers switch subjects so rapidly, but gradually I'm getting on to it.

Jake informed me today that he is leaving soon for good. He's going to the India, China Wing. Major John Proven asked for him and Col. Farley said he could go. Of course I won't believe all of this until he's actually on the plane. Jake has a good imagination. Naturally I think this decision has a lot to do with my refusal to marry him and my disavowed love for him. I'm sorry this is so. I would have liked him to have made the decision freely.

I want to go to Church this weekend, I feel the need. Mrs. Nelson goes every Sunday and she brings little cakes for after services. I'm going to ask her if I can join her. I think she'll like that. Maybe I can help her serve the coffee and cakes.

Saturday, February 13, 1943

I met Jake downtown in the pouring rain. We got beautifully drenched. We had dinner and then went to the movies. It was my second time seeing "Casablanca" and did I adore it. Jake gave me my Valentine present a head of time, a bottle of Mais Oui Perfume. It is too delicious for words.

Robert had asked me if I would meet him for a cocktail after 10:00 at the Mayflower bar. I did so not want to lie to Jake, but I had to spare his feelings. After all, he made such a beautiful evening for me tonight.

Robert was waiting for me at the bar and appeared to be a bit annoyed that I was late. I shared Jake's news with Robert about his leaving. His mood changed and he was very sympathetic.

Sunday, February 14, 1943
Valentine's Day

I was too tired to make it to church with Mrs. Nelson. I feel a little guilty. I think she was looking forward to it.

It's a sunny day, but bitterly cold out. I received two dozen red roses from "Lord Nelson." Their beauty is so typical of his love. I had to tell the girls, and Jake that the flowers were from Mother and Dad. It's not really fair that my dearest friends can't know of my good fortune to have such a wonderful and charming Valentine.

Jake got back from a short trip he had to take. He bought me Chinese lounging pajamas, so gorgeous, satin damask in maroon with silver flowers. He also got me an air force, sterling silver identification bracelet. They are very popular. Everyone has one.

Monday, February 15, 1943

My darling and I had dinner and then he took me right home because I have come down with the sniffles, not feeling 100%. He couldn't see me to the door, who knows who might be watching.

Jake tucked me in to bed. I guess I shouldn't let him do those things. Last night he told me that his insurance is to be divided between his sister and I if he is killed - also air pay when his insurance is to be divided. I don't really know how I should feel about that. I don't want to think about something happening to him. My heart would break if something ... I refuse to finish the thought.

As though he could read my mind Jake came into my bedroom with a hot cup of tea with lemon and some of Mrs. Nelson's Irish whiskey. We'll have to chip in and buy her another bottle. He sat with me for a while, then he waited for me to fall asleep before he left.

Wednesday, February 17, 1943

I worked a little late for my adored "Lord Nelson." I do hope that I don't end up as tragically as Lady Hamilton did. She died penniless and very much alone. I can't image that Robert would ever allow that to happen to me.

After we finished working we had dinner at the Watergate Inn and then he took me to a wonderful concert at Constitution Hall. Neither of us had ever been there before. Jose Iturbi was the soloist. He's master of the keyboard. The last part of the program was the best, Waltzes from Der Rosenkavalier. We thrilled to the music at the same time, truly a meeting of minds and souls. I tried to imagine dancing with Robert across a beautiful ballroom, he in a dark black tux, and I in a shimmering silver ball gown.

Friday, February 19, 1943

I took notes at a big meeting in the Munitions building. When I am old and gray I shall remember these days when I saw and watched secret war plans being made. All of these men have such trust in me. This is such an honor to be in the same room with such powerful military minds. It seems as though my life is built on keeping secrets. It's a very difficult way to live. I have to be on my guard at all times.

My darling and I had dinner afterwards and he divulged intimate pages from his past life, for which I love him all the more.

He handed me a box and in it I found the most beautiful identification bracelet I've ever seen, for me to give Jake. It does not have the Air Forces insignia so I will show it to him and see if he would like it engraved. This is how wonderful Robert is. He wanted me to have a nice parting gift for Jake. I should have thought of it myself.

When I got home the girls were waiting up for me. We haven't spent much time together. Kate had made chicken and rice, which I had missed, as I was dining with my beloved. I felt a little guilty so I stayed up with them and played Society Craps. I ended up feeling even guiltier because I won 67 cents.

I can't wait to sleep in tomorrow. Saturday is my favorite day of the week. I have the entire day to myself to spend as I please. As fate would have it, just before I went to bed Jake knocked on my door and asked if we could spend some time together. How could I say no?

Saturday, February 20, 1943

The smell of bacon, eggs, toast and coffee was intoxicating this morning. Mrs. Nelson is such a dear.

It felt like a real spring day today. Jake and I strolled by Rock Creek and walked down to the Lusitania Memorial by the river. This has been a day to remember. I actually think my Jake will be leaving.

Monday, February 22, 1943
Washington's Birthday

I can remember the good old days of peace when everyone had this day off. I Wonder what General Washington would say if he could come back now? I like to think of him as a general, a soldier, rather than a politician.

Air amphibian meeting today. I took some very interesting notes. My darling and I worked tonight and then stayed in the car while the blackout was on. It was divine. Words cannot describe the ecstasy. Home is where Robert and I are together. How wondrous is this fact! There are not many people in this world who have a sanctuary they can always depend upon. We don't have the luxury of dreaming about a home of our own. I am content, for now, with what he has to offer.

Tuesday, February 23, 1943

Robert and I went to The Munitions Building and left some papers for a Lt. Rogers. We walked by the river to the Watergate Inn and had an excellent chicken barbeque dinner. Then we went to the concert at Constitution Hall. Efren Zimbalist the violinist was guest artist. He played violin concerto by Tchaikovsky. It was enhralling to say the least.

No one appears to take notice of us being out together all of the time. They must think he's being kind to me because I am so young and so far away from home. I'm sure that is part of it, but little do they know of our secret love. Sometimes secrets can be exciting.

Monday, March 1, 1943

Mrs. Miller has some exciting news of her own. She has a steady job at the War Department at Arlington Hall. She's very excited because she's going to go to school to learn her duties. She has always wanted to help in the war effort in some way, and now this is her chance.

Robert and I went to dinner at the Hot Shoppe for burgers and shakes. He told me a great deal about when he attended West Point and his life there. It contributed a great deal to the man he is today.

I believe he is a great man in the true sense of the word. No one will ever know this of course. It won't be written in the history books, but it is men like Robert who contribute to the onward march of civilization.

God is being very good to us. I wonder if he really planned all this. I don't see how Robert can be as perfect as he is. Looking at him hurts sometimes. He is so gentle, wise and adorable. Someday I hope I can tell mother all about this. She'd understand, but no one else would.

Manuel phoned while I was out.

Tuesday, March 2, 1943

The following is secret, but no one will ever read this diary until after the war is over: The Air Amphibian Committee is now engaged in the writing of a Communication Doctrine for Air Amphibian Operations and combined operation signal book. The deadline for drafts is March 10. I'm the only person in the room who isn't Military upper echelon. We are going to be working very hard over the next week or so. I'm ready.

Robert and I went to the concert of the Philadelphia Orchestra with Eugene Ormandy conducting. Quite a lot of modern music on the program. It was beautiful and exciting to listen to. I don't believe Robert enjoyed it as much as I did. He said he prefers the classics.

Friday, March 5, 1943

Jake woke me up this morning and showed me his travel orders. He'll be in Las Vegas now for a few days before he leaves for India. He's getting a five day delay in Fort Worth so he can see his friends there.

My darling and I worked tonight until eleven o'clock. This Air Amphibian Committee is really putting out the work. It's so quiet and sometimes a little frightening in this building so late at night. Sometimes it's like a creaky old house, making the most unusual sounds. It's a very powerful place, you can almost feel its heart beating, and hear it breathing. It truly is haunting.

I should write to Mother tonight, and I'll put a note in for Dad. I miss them at times like this. I miss the comfort they would shower me with. I also want them to know that I am safe. I feel very safe with Robert.

Saturday, March 6, 1943

Jake and I saw our last movie together "Air Force" with John Garfield and Gig Young. How very ironic. I made sure to wear the Air Force heart he gave me. The movie was superb. This is the beginning of his send off. I don't like not knowing what is going to happen to him. I wish I could make him feel safe.

Sunday, March 7, 1943

I worked for a couple of hours, but should have worked all day. Robert knew I wanted to be with Jake before he left. Mrs. Nelson had a corned beef dinner a la buffet for Jake tonight. It was all rather quiet, the three of us sitting there. I'm not sure what Mrs. Nelson thinks Jake's and my relationship is. I rather think she feels we're very close. I do wear the heart he gave me on special occasions. I told him it was too flashy to wear all the time. I do, however, wear Robert's hearts.

Monday, March 8, 1943

This was a real memory day. We worked from 7:00 a.m. until 3:30. Robert let me drive his car to the station. Jake and I had an hour before train time. We had cocktails, there was music playing, "Easy to Love" was one of the numbers. How true those lyrics are. Jake is so easy to love, I'm just not sure how deeply I could let myself fall for him. We were very quiet and Jake was nicer than ever before. He kissed me about fifteen times and when the train pulled out, he was crying.

Worked until 10:00 p.m., called Mother and Dad.

Wednesday, March 10, 1943

I felt very sad and lonely all day. Robert is so comforting always. I guess I'm lonely for Jake because it was just as though we were married, him tucking me into bed, bringing me orange juice on Sunday mornings, calling me up every day at work, just to check in and see what I was doing that night. I expected him to call tonight from Fort Worth.

Thursday, March 11, 1943

This is a great day. The Joint Communication Board approved the "Communication Doctrine for Combined Air Amphibian Operations." It is most gratifying to Robert and the other members of the committee who composed the document. I hope the British concur. The party has already left for London.

I went shopping today and bought a blue "fascinator." It's such a darling little hat. I saw Rosalind Russell wear one in her last movie. Mother wants me to send her ideas for birthday presents. There are so many things I could use. I'll have to make time to sit down and write out a list. It makes it much easier for her.

Robert and I had dinner at The Watergate Inn. We sat and chatted about our day, just like an old married couple. What would I ever do without him?

Friday, March 12, 1943

Tonight Robert took his daughter Lily and myself to Olmstead for dinner and then to see "Priorities of 1943," a stage show at the National. The show was just fair, but it was a thoroughly enjoyable evening. I wore my blue dress with the rhinestone leaf clip that Robert gave me on my jacket.

I came home to find a note for me saying to call operator 125 in Fort Worth. Talking to Jake was a thrill supreme. When he said, "I love you," my heart missed a beat.

Saturday, March 13, 1943

It was pouring rain this morning. I was thankful to have Robert call for me. I thought of Jake all day long. He has left an indelible mark on my heart forever. Jake and I would laugh so much together, and play silly games. Being with him was always so simple and uncomplicated.

I parked in Arlington Cemetery after working a few hours for Robert. I cried for about two hours over Jake. I didn't really think I would feel this way when Jake left. I had talked so much of it through with Robert and I thought I knew where my feelings were. But now I'm not so sure. It's as though my heart is trying to tell me something and my mind keeps pushing those thoughts away.

Robert said I am "paying the piper" for the intimate life I shared with Jake. Could that really be true?

Monday, March 15, 1943

I had just got in bed last night when a knock came to my door. Mrs. Nelson brought up a special delivery letter from Jake. It was a lovely letter ending with those heart throbbing words, "I love you." This morning I received two more letters from Jake. He says he dare not think of how much he will miss me when he leaves the country.

Robert took me to see "Random Harvest" with Ronald Coleman and Greer Garson, it was beautiful. Miss Garson's character loved Ronald Coleman's character so much. She never gave up on him.

I lay in bed tonight, another emotional session with my heart. Confusion over Jake still exists. Time, I suppose, will heal the memory of Jake. What I must guard against is the building of a halo around him. Absence makes you forget a person's short comings and thus a mirage occurs. My first letter to Jake must be just right.

I have been having a terrible time getting to sleep. Robert said that he could get some sleeping tablets for me if I need them. He said that I have to be very careful and only take them when I really need a good night sleep. I don't really want to do that. I remember there was a time when Mother would take them and she was so groggy the next day.

I have such confusion in my heart and mind. I've been wearing Jake's heart when Robert won't see it. I keep it with me always. Jake is my friend too. He's not just someone who I kiss and make love to, he's someone who I laugh with, someone who takes care of me and I take care of him. Oh my heart.

Monday, March 22, 1943

I have received six letters from Jake all pouring his heart out to me and professing his undying love. What to do? What to feel?

With all of my own romantic endeavors I haven't been paying much attention to Jackie and Kate. Both girls seem to be content playing the field. We haven't heard from Harry in ages. We were all dateless tonight so decided to go see the new Hitchcock move, "Shadow of a Doubt." What a thriller! It's all about a man who garners great respect, but in the end turns out to be a murderer.

Then we came home and compared notes about our lives. This is such a difficult time to be a young woman. Everything was all figured out for women like my mother when she was my age. I wish I could share everything with my friends.

Wednesday, March 24, 1943

I am hearing regularly from Jake. He is surely faithful. I wonder how long he will keep it up. He should have gotten my letter today. I had a long talk with Robert regarding my confusion and doubts about life. It helps, but never fully erases the clouds in my mind.

I bought a darling little tea set at an antique shop today, cream with small dark pink roses. I saw it in a shop window and thought it would be fun for the girls and me to have tea on Sunday afternoons. There are four cups and saucers, one for each of us and a guest.

Did some washing and got a letter off to Jake.

Friday, March 26, 1943

I picked up my identification bracelet that Jake gave me. The engraving looks swell. I still miss him terribly. Robert bought me a beautiful yellow blouse. We had dinner at the Little Tea House over on South Arlington Ridge Road. I had mentioned my new tea set to Robert and he immediately thought of taking me to the Tea House, what a darling. It was delicious and we had a table with a view overlooking a bluff. We loved tonight down by the Tidal Basin.

Received another letter from Jake.

Tuesday, March 30, 1943

Received three more letters from Jake. He sent me a darling bandana from Las Vegas. I find myself thinking of Jake all the time - even when I'm with Robert. This is all very confusing to me. Where is the way out?

Robert and I started out to work, but I was troubled and it was such a lovely day we took a ride down Mt. Vernon Drive by the river. We parked and sat on a log on the sand. It was beautiful. He held my hand and my thumb rubbed over his wedding ring. I commented that it seemed to be on so tight. And he said, "Not all that tight."

Wednesday, April 7, 1943

I continue to get letters from Jake. I can't seem to get him off my mind. That's bad too. I need to move on. Today was very warm. The blossoms are out, grass is green and buds are on the trees. It's great to be alive.

I think I'll take a walk by myself today.

Thursday, April 8, 1943

War News:

We are still being fooled by optimistic headlines.

Robert had some professional photographs taken. The miniature one is mine to look at forever, the larger ones are for his family. I keep it in my bed stand drawer and give it a quick kiss goodnight before I retire. Someday I would like to have a framed photograph of my love to place by my bed instead of the publicity photo of George Brent. The girls have kidded me from time to time. It does seem a bit childish to have a movie star photo framed and in my room. Perhaps the small photo he gave me will give me courage in some dark hour of the future.

What a difference a day makes. I was so full of hope yesterday. The cherry blossoms don't hold the joy they did for me yesterday. In the deep blue night they show up in stark loveliness beside the Tidal Basin. Washington - the city of searing beauty and wretched cruelty.

Friday, April 9, 1943

I had two letters from Jake. As yet his group hasn't been paid. He has his eye on a birthday present for me. Life is certainly lonely without him. I guess I miss him more for what he did for me than what he is. He's so in love with me, it hurts beyond belief sometimes.

Tonight Robert took me to see "The Student Prince" with Everett Marshall, famous baritone. It was just as lovely as Mother and Dad told me long ago. The singing was so beautiful it twisted my heart practically in two. In fact, I cried from the middle to the end. Robert was equally affected, his arm trembled several times. The operetta only makes me realize how much I really love Robert.

These are such happy days we have together. I hope their memory will suffice to tide us over the lonely years ahead. We drove out to a secluded road near the Army Navy Club after the Operetta. The moon and stars were out, so beautiful, so clear you could reach out and touch them. We loved, and it was so beautiful. No woman before in the history of time has ever known a fuller love or more ecstasy than I.

When I got home Jake called me very late from Las Vegas. Mrs. Nelson was perturbed, I could tell. His voice was so good to hear. He adores me so, I wish I could say, "I love you." I'm so happy; Jake says he hopes to get here on furlough. To think, if I hadn't come to Washington, I would never have known all this life, for that is what this all is.

Sunday, April 11, 1943

Jake called me at work today from Las Vegas. It was our last time to talk, for he received orders to proceed into the great unknown. His voice was stronger than usual. It was as though he was protecting me from what he will be facing. He wanted me to know that he was ready for this ultimate challenge. His furlough is not to be.

Monday, April 12, 1943

The girls can see how upset I am about Jake. They know I have feelings for him. Perhaps they know my mind better than I.

Maureen and I had dinner together and then went to the movies. We saw an excellent movie, "The Hard Way." We talked about the war and decided people living by the "golden rule" would insure peace from now on. Of course, that will never happen.

Jake is sending me a ring for my birthday. I made sure it wasn't an engagement ring. I wouldn't want to accept anything binding.

Friday, April 16, 1943

Jake sent me a card postmarked Carbondale, Illinois. I can't make out the delivery route to reach his ultimate destination.

I had dinner tonight at Olmstead with Robert and Col. Seward, he was as charming a young man as I've ever met. He would make the ideal husband, but alas he is already married.

We worked a while tonight. When Robert kisses me his lips tremble. There can be nothing lovelier in life.

Saturday, April 17, 1943

Jake called me from West Palm Beach. He's made his last will and testament and left everything to me. What a dear boy he is. The ring arrived. It is lovely, very simple and in good taste.

Mother and Dad sent me a new dress, a skirt to match one of my blouses, a blue slip and a check for $5.00. They are such loving and kind parents. I hope that they know how much I appreciate them and all that they do for me. I am blessed to have so many people who love me so much.

Sunday, April 18, 1943
My 23 Birthday

This birthday is a real memory day. Robert had five presents hidden in the conference room for me. A set of toiletries, a real silk nightie, slip and panties, a gorgeous cigarette case and compact to match and a blue hostess apron trimmed in lace.

When I got home from work there was a special delivery letter from Jake waiting for me. His will was enclosed. Naturally I am highly complimented. What woman wouldn't be! I showed the will to Robert, and it presents quite a few problems. I must write to Jake's sister Helen. It is the only fair thing to do.

Jake put a check call through to me and I was home at 7:00 to receive it, after dining at Pierre's with Robert. Jake says he is living the life of Riley down in Miami. I'm glad. He expects to be there a couple of days. I wrote him a long letter with a splitting headache. It was interrupted by a sudden storm of hail. Stones so big a man was knocked down outside. I mailed the letter and hope it gets there late tomorrow.

Wednesday, April 21, 1943

This departure of Jake is becoming prolonged. He called me at the office believing it to be the last time. In a guarded way he said departure would take place tonight. So be it. How I wish I could have said, "I love you." Only the Lord above knows the end of all of this and I should not worry about it.

Robert and I had dinner together at the Little Tea House. We came back to the Pentagon made love a little and talked a lot. He tries to help me in my confusion.

Friday, April 30, 1943

My cousin Carol came for a visit from Buffalo and I went down to the station to meet her. As I expected, a sailor was carrying her bags. She was bubbling over with news, so we went into the lounge and had highballs. We really got to know each other's ideas, hopes, loves, etc. It is truly grand having a grown up cousin now to talk to. She has gone through much the same experiences that I have. She's staying in my room with me. I'm so happy to have someone from home to visit.

I took Carol to see Mt. Vernon. I saw more than I saw the first time. Of course I was quite preoccupied the first time, with my loves arms around me. It is a spot out of heaven. I so enjoyed showing her around. There is so much to see. I like to think about how Martha Washington went from room to room deciding what furniture would go where and the colors and fabrics. How wonderful it must be to decorate your own home.

We went to The Watergate Inn for dinner. Carol was duly impressed. After dinner we went to the movies to see Spencer Tracy and Katherine Hepburn in "Keeper of the Flame." It was a surprising movie and superbly acted.

Tuesday, May 4, 1943
War News:

I recall that I haven't said anything about the war in a long time. We have won the Battle of Tunisia - the first step on a long road to victory.

I received a card with Jake's PO number. Robert is going to try to see where he is located for me.

Carol had the good fortune to see the Supreme Court in session and said she felt like she was in a Frank Capra movie. She said that it was so moving to see democracy in action. She stayed there for hours and couldn't pull herself away.

All that democracy gave Carol a headache tonight and she had to beg off on dinner. Robert and I dined at the Little Tea House. Afterward we found our nook in Arlington and made love. It was more than glorious. What a glowing memory it will all be some day.

We sat in the car and watched the sun set. Jake is becoming a lovely memory to me now.

Saturday, May 8, 1943

Carol left on the 2:00 p.m. train. Robert took her to lunch and put her on the train himself. It was too sad for me to say goodbye to her at the station. They had a long confidential talk. Robert set her straight on a lot of things and I hope she absorbed them fully.

Robert and I dined at Jene's tonight. I was dying for some Italian food and it's so romantic there. The tables have blue and white checked table clothes with Chianti bottles with candles in them. Dinner by candlelight is my favorite. After dinner we rode out along the Potomac and sat by the river, moon shining through the

93

trees, soft breeze, and me, snuggling up to Robert. He is family to me here.

Wednesday, May 19, 1943

War News:

Churchill addressed a joint session of Congress. He praised the partnership of the two Allies. On the 17th the Germans launched their fifth major offensive against Tito's partisans in Yugoslavia.

Today is Mother's birthday. I hope she received the cigarette case on time.

I bought some white gauntlet gloves, stockings, and a new purse. I had steak at Herzog's tonight with Robert. We are so deeply in love. What will life be like after the day of separation? I dare not think.

I made up my own birthday card for Jake, even stapled some sergeant stripes on it. I hope he gets to use them. I received two letters from Jake today. It's a beautiful spot where he is, but the boys work very hard, seven days a week. They are up at 5:30 and to bed at eight or nine. I do wish they were given some time off. Jake says his love for me grows deeper as each day passes. He really has his heart set on winning me. How I wish he could be the one after this war is over.

Monday, May 31, 1943

We worked on the Amphibian Conference. Words cannot express what it is like to be sitting in the same room with the man I love every day.

I received six letters from Jake, all more or less in the same vein. He's working so hard and misses me desperately. I am so worried.

He's over there dreaming up plans for the future with me in it. I hope time solves all of this.

The weather is terribly hot. It hits you like a stone wall upon emerging from the Pentagon. Robert and I had our usual dish of country cooked chicken at the Little Tea House. We made love tonight. We never can resist.

Saturday, June 5, 1943

Tonight I began my first weekend with a man in another city, the man I love. I met Robert in Baltimore. We are staying at the Belvedere. It's a beautiful hotel. I swept into the lobby with my dark blue suit on. I felt so confident and mature.

We went to a night club tonight, Club Charles. There was a great floor show. We are going to bed now. I know I shall never forget. I love it that I can reach out and touch him. This is heavenly. Although, I have not been possessed, it is as if I were because now I can never erase the memory of Robert. I am living in this wonderful dream, yet I know, some day it will crash.

Tuesday, June 8, 1943

I was very depressed all day thinking about us. Robert is most understanding and does his best to help me wrestle with my problem. So often I wish I were back in Buffalo with a life of peace and security. But then, when I think of giving up Robert the idea is horrifying. Oh Robert, I love you so desperately. Does Jake love me that way? I wonder? His letters are full of his love. But is it the same?

Saturday, June 12, 1943
The Watergate Inn

I received a more optimistic letter from Jake than usual. I guess it is pretty exciting over there. Robert and I worked from 2:00 to 6:00 and dined at the Watergate Inn, then worked some more from

8:00 to 9:00. The sunset was beautiful after a storm, most awe inspiring heat lightening I've ever seen.

I wrote Mother and Dad tonight. There is so much going on in my life that they know nothing about. I have never held anything back from them and it hurts me to do so. I don't feel ashamed. A love like this could never be shameful. I simply don't like having an abyss between my parents and myself. I want them to know how much their daughter is adored.

Robert is such a generous and kind man. He bought some ties for me to give dad for Father's Day. He is always thinking about me and what would make me happy.

Tonight Kate and I went to see Tyrone Power in "Crash Dive" glorifying the submarine hero's. It was swell but depicted the good side only. Tyrone Power is the most beautiful man I have ever seen. Of course I will always have a soft spot for Errol Flynn, and George Brent, who looks so much like Robert it makes my heart skip a beat.

Monday, June 21, 1943

War News:

Operation Cartwheel opens with landings by our Marine Raider Battalion at Sega Point on New Georgia in the Solomon Islands, beginning the New Georgia Campaign.

I sat for three hours revising the communications instructions for amphibian operations. It is going to be a big job. In addition to that, Robert is getting out mainstream notes on field artillery radio equipment, what a job!

Tonight Robert and I were so hot and tired we rode out in Virginia and parked. We lay on a blanket and watched a rainstorm come up. It was truly sublime. I came home to find a present from Jake. A ring, an aquamarine set in gold and a pin and earring set of India silver, so delicate. I immediately wrote Jake a thank you.

Monday, August 9, 1943

I simply haven't had the interest to sit down and write in my diary the last several weeks. Many things have happened. Jake has been very ill with a high fever. They may be sending him home. I have no idea what I will do when, and if, that occurs.

Robert went on an extended trip with his family and I stayed at his home to take care of their cat. I felt that I was in the home that should be ours, but never will be I know.

Robert asked if I would pick them up from the station as I have been enjoying the use of their car; our car, the car where we have loved in so many times.

I had to put my mind in another place when I pulled into the station and saw him standing there on the platform with his family.

The kids have a tan and look fine. Mrs. Munton, although 43, doesn't look a day over 28. She thanked me for picking them up and then asked if I would like to join them for dinner. We all decided on the Hot Shoppe, Robert's and my favorite spot.

The family could never guess that I was in love with Robert. I acted so natural.

Monday, August 16, 1943

I haven't slept in days. The heat is unbearable and my thoughts and fears invade my mind with an unrelenting force. I am at battle with myself. Robert is truly a wonderful person guiding me through my blue moods and fears for the future. Naturally I wouldn't want to know what's going to happen to me.

However, I do get frantic sometimes knowing I can't have Robert. Any other man will be second choice. I feel sure of that.

Four packages arrived from Jake. There was a delicate ivory bracelet, a silver and a gold chain bracelet, and a silver cross on a chain. I thought it was so touching of him to give me that cross. He's a very devout Catholic and I know it holds great significance to him. It may even be his mother's. He also enclosed a lovely ivory necklace for Mother.

The Irish are indeed a very romantic and sentimental people. He always tells me how much his mother would have liked me.

Saturday, August 28, 1943

I've been able to take some time off, as my Grammie is not doing very well. I took the train back to Buffalo to see her. I hope it won't be for the last time. I sat on her bed and she looked so frail and thin, not at all her old self. She gave me some old photos of Dad when he was a boy in buckled boots and scratchy wool. Poor Dad.

I confided to Grammie that I was anticipating somewhat of an impending broken heart. I couldn't tell her more. Somehow I could feel that she knew what I was saying. She told me that I should guard my heart, but don't imprison it.

Tuesday, August 31, 1943

I rather expected a letter today from Robert, but was disappointed. Sitting down at our piano gave me a warm and comforting feeling. I have only played one selection since I've been home, Grieg's Concerto. It's beautiful, but it makes me so sad. I think about Robert all the time. It is overpowering. The mail man finally rang the doorbell and there was the letter that I knew would come. I had to tell Mother and Dad it was from Jackie. I do so dislike the pretense.

Friday, September 10, 1943

A new blow for me. Jackie has decided to move home. I did not see this coming. Expenses have become too much for her. I am going to miss her terribly. I tried so hard to convince her to stay. I know she could get a better paying job. Perhaps Col. Munton could find a job for her. I don't think I'll be able to change her mind. She seems determined to leave.

The house is becoming so empty. Jake is gone, now Jackie. Mrs. Nelson wants to keep Jake's room open for him for a while. What a kind and generous thing for her to do. She wants to make sure he has somewhere to come home to as we have all become his family. She became quite fond of him. We all did.

I'm sure Mrs. Nelson is going to want to get another girl in the house to take Jackie's place. I'm more than a little worried about that.

Monday, September 13, 1943

I have so much personal stuff lately to deal with that progress of war hasn't been noted. There has been heavy fighting in Italy. Nazis are trying to hold north and allies are on their way up the "boot".

Oh lovely day. Robert and I took a long walk around the lagoon in front of the Pentagon and down the river. Perfect for walking. I told him of my worries about a new girl coming into the house. Dear, dear Robert made a lovely and generous suggestion. He offered to pay Jackie's portion of the rent. And he suggested that I talk to Mrs. Nelson and Kate about having Kate live in Jake's old room. As long as it's just sitting up there empty, why not have Kate enjoy some privacy. Oh to have the entire room to myself, what luxury.

The leaves are beginning to change ever so slightly. It's always so sad when summer comes to an end. There is an eerie coolness in the air that runs through me. I do so hope that it is not an omen of things to come.

Saturday, September 18, 1943

Moving day! We put Jackie on the bus last night after a lovely dinner put on by Mrs. Nelson. She invited Mrs. Miller over and we enjoyed Mrs. Nelson's beef stew and homemade biscuits. We even had some apple pie. It was rather subdued as we were all sad to see Jackie leaving us. I know we'll keep in touch.

It was quite a job moving things around, but Kate is thrilled to have her own room and it looks so lovely.

As I went to bed tonight it was so still in our room, no giggling or sounds of whispering. This added to my already blue mood. I worry about the future. I try so hard not to, but thoughts keep creeping in to my mind.

It's all so silly really. What a comfort Robert is. His understanding goes beyond mortal ability.

Saturday, September 25, 1943

Very strange and out of the ordinary occurrence at the house. Mrs. Nelson has gone out of her head; she appears to have a persecution complex and hasn't eaten anything in three days. She confided in me that she has had these attacks before. How odd that I have never noticed. Is it because there is only the three of us living in the house? I wonder.

I'd like to go to church with her tomorrow, but Robert asked me to come to work. He needs me to help him. He didn't mention what it was about, but I'm sure it must be important. I'll try to go to church with her next week. And I will say a prayer for her tonight. I'm sure she'll be fine. Robert and I had dinner at the Watergate Inn then went to see "This is the Army" a grand show with a great many nostalgic tunes.

We made love in the Buick - so beautiful, how can we ever part?

Sunday, September 26, 1943

Robert's children, Lily and Carl came over to the Pentagon and I took them around the building. We saw the Secretary of War's dining room all set for dinner. Robert  took us over to the Army show on the Washington Monument grounds. Lovely day. We worked for four hours. Then Robert took a picture of me sitting in the car. I call it the "love" mobile.

Crown Restaurant
517 - 13TH N. W. WASHINGTON, D. C.

We had dinner at the Watergate Inn and then went for a ride. We love each other more every day, if that's possible. Robert suggested that we cut down on our lunches and start taking daily walks instead. He also suggested my eating less bread and perhaps eating more vegetables and no more sweets for me for a while. He said my weight is too much for a little girl like me. He's always looking out for my best interests.

I read The Great Gatsby last night. Daisy is such an interesting character. I couldn't really tell if she loved Gatsby or not. There were many parts where she seemed desperately in love, but at the end there was so little emotion from her.

Monday September 27, 1943

I took notes at a committee meeting which was difficult, very secret subject. Robert said I did excellently, which thrilled me.

I went shopping and bought two Christmas presents, a blouse and pretty clothes hamper for my room. I received a letter from Mother today. I've been trying to convince her to come and visit me, especially since I have the room all to myself now. I know she will put plenty of obstacles in the way, mainly the strain on the budget. I could really use a visit from her. I know she would have a wonderful time.

Being all alone in our room now seems so lonely. Kate comes in some nights and we'll play cards but it's not really the same. The house is so quiet. I miss how full the house used to be with Jake and Jackie and all of the soldiers coming in and out.

I went to the U.S. Rubber Exhibition for the Army & Navy at the Mayflower Hotel. It was superb. Rubber is now being used as a conductor of electricity, something I never knew before.

101

My love and I dined at The Crown on 13th NW. Lovely dinner until one gentleman made an exhibition of himself by talking too loud and having to be escorted out. It was obvious that he was inebriated. Robert and I discussed the evils of drink. After having witnessed such a scene I am soured on night clubs and excessive drinking. I must add however, that Robert and I are very careful not to over indulge. A man in uniform represents his country, and Robert is fully aware of this. He is a high ranking officer, and a gentleman.

"Sunshine" and I worked again tonight. I have never spent so much time working before and loving it too in the bargain.

Robert made a suggestion tonight. He asked me if Mrs. Nelson was a light sleeper. I didn't know how to answer that. She would ask us to keep it down when we'd have gab fests in our room and laugh quite loudly. Then, of course, sometimes a tank could roll through the house and she wouldn't wake up. I wonder what my Robert has in mind. Wink.

I'll have to have a key made for him tomorrow and give it to him as a surprise. We'll have to be very careful. Especially with how odd Mrs. Nelson has been.

Saturday, October 2, 1943

I went out with Col. Denton. He's just come in from having been stationed in London. We dined and danced at the Lotus Club.

He wanted to show me his apartment, but I declined as a lady should, amid many protests from him. I have to admit, I was just a little tempted, but only a little.

We went out to the airport. Out on the observation platform I met Kay Crafts, now a WAC. I went to secretarial school with her in Buffalo and haven't seen her since. I probably never would have met up with her had I not gone out tonight.

Robert and I worked hard on drawing diagrams for the Amphibious Communications Instructions. You almost get cross-eyed. The one thing that keeps you going is the knowledge of the importance of the work. No amphibious operation can be successful without our work. Something to write home about some day.

We needed something to get our minds off this arduous work. We went to see Gary Cooper and Ingrid Bergman in "For Whom the Bell Tolls." It is from Ernest Hemingway's book on the Spanish Civil War. It was a powerful movie and terribly sad. The acting was superb. I was weak at the finish. Should have seen a comedy.

When I got home I received a call from a girl whose husband is in India with Jake. He was in the hospital with him. The hospital is in Karachi which is on the Western coast of India. The girl's name was Beverly and her husband's name was Jake too. She wants to know if we could meet for dinner some night soon. I would love to hear how my Jake is doing. She said that Jake and her husband have become very good friends. She said they are both very in love, and then she giggled a little.

I didn't sleep very well tonight. I woke up in a hot sweat. I can't remember what I was dreaming about, but I couldn't get back to sleep. I felt so anxious and worried.

Friday, October 8, 1943

I took Beverly to dinner at the Hot Shoppe. She is just a kid, only eighteen and so in love with her Jake. I was eager to hear how my Jake was doing. She said that he is doing much better and that he wanted her to get in touch with me to put my mind at ease. She said he's been worried because he hasn't heard from me. What could I say to this child? How could I tell her that I'm in love with another man?

Tuesday, October 12, 1943

Robert and I have reached an impasse tonight. He hasn't understood me for the past ten days. He was terribly distressed and I was too, because sometimes I can't understand myself either.

I wrote a letter to Grammie. I told her how very sad and worried I am. Perhaps I shouldn't have, but she understands me so. She always has.

Kate and I needed a night on the town. We went to a new place called The Windsor Room. We had cocktails and I had a lobster. The piano player and singer were excellent and group singing was in order. It felt so good not to have to think about anything of real importance. Even though we didn't know anyone who gathered around the piano it felt as though we were all good friends. Gee it was fun. I really needed it.

Sometimes I think I'm too young for all of this heart ache and uncertainty. I just don't know.

Wednesday, October 13, 1943

I love Robert so deeply. How I would adore having a child of his. No doubt that will never come to pass. Life cannot grant you everything. This love of ours is miracle enough.

I received a card from Aunt Millie saying that Grammie passed away night before last. She never got to read my letter. Perhaps that is for the best.

I feel so sorry for my Daddy. He was away on business and never got there in time. I hope not seeing his mother doesn't haunt him. I'm feeling very anxious again. I miss home and all that I know and trust.

This time of year is so haunting. The moon is so full and bright at night. The moon shines over all of us, Robert, Jake and me.

Monday, October 18, 1943

Today was Robert's 20th wedding anniversary. He gave Mrs. Munton some lovely presents. He also gave me a good sized bottle of Ciro's "Danger" perfume. It is very siren-ish.

I came home to find two letters from Jake. He is still in the hospital. He said not to mail him his Christmas present because it might get lost in route. It's too late now because I mailed it four days ago.

Tuesday, October 19, 1943

Gosh I was blue all day. Its Robert's teasing in the office that gets me. I just can't take it sometimes, because I love him so much I guess. I want to tell the world I love him, but of course that's too impractical. He is so dear to me, so gentle and understanding. No one but me knows how much.

I received a grand letter from Mother. She is actually considering a trip here. She says all she needs is some good nerve pills. She said that Dad is doing well and not to worry about him.

Monday, October 25, 1943

Robert told me he has received an offer to be on General Marshall's staff in London when he becomes Commander of the Allied Armies. However, he feels he is doing the war effort a lot more good here. What a scare for me.

Friday, October 29, 1943

Tonight the office had a party at the Lotus Club. The occasion was Mabel's 21st birthday. She's a girl who works for Col. Morris. She had her first drink, a daiquiri on my recommendation.

Robert and Mrs. Munton were there and some of the officers. Dancing with Robert was perfect, but not enough of it. We conceal our love admirably in public. We just kid and banter around royally.

I wrote to Jake tonight. It's amazing how much his letters have dropped off. Natural though. The old times and space idea.

Friday, October 29, 1943

Robert went to Monmouth on temporary leave. I am to join him tomorrow night in Philly.

Saturday, October 30, 1943

I met Robert at the station in Philly. He looks wonderful, so happy to see me. He booked us a room at the Philadelphian #857. Our love was passion filled and endless. How can this man be 43?

We went out for dinner and Robert confided in me how worried he is about his daughter Lily. He and Mrs. Munton are having trouble with her. She is growing up very fast and thinks Robert and Mrs. Munton are too strict with her. She promises to be home at a certain time and then doesn't keep her word.

Tomorrow I have to take the 8:10 train back to D.C. I don't want to leave #857.

Friday, November 5, 1943

Robert and I went to the Watergate Inn for dinner. Col. Denton was there with a young woman, another gal in his collection.

I haven't heard from Jake in a couple of weeks. He may be moving back to his station or maybe coming back here. We'll have to change the rooms around again. I don't know what it will be like to have Jake back in the house again.

Robert has been enjoying sneaking in at night. Unfortunately, we may have to return to the "Love Mobile."

Monday, November 8, 1943

The paper tonight says all holiday leaves are out. However, Christmas comes on Saturday this year so I plan to take the sleeper Christmas Eve and come back to Washington Sunday night. I pray that I'll be able to get my train reservation.

Monday, November 15, 1943

Robert and Mrs. Munton are going to Roanoke to see Robert's mother the day after Thanksgiving. I am to stay with the kids all that weekend. I am thrilled with the idea of playing "mother" for a while. Robert says Lily is all excited.

I got home to find a letter from Jake waiting. As I suspected he is coming home for treatment and rest. My life is going to be very conflicted once he gets back to the States.

Thursday, November 18, 1943

I wrapped Christmas presents, one thing I never tire of doing. Mrs. Nelson, Kate and I played Society Craps tonight. I'm usually the big winner, but lost 56 cents. I didn't have my mind in the game I guess. Yesterday was Robert's and my first anniversary - and I forgot it.

Friday, November 19, 1943

I have turned in 33 hours of overtime for cash which will come in nicely. I worked a little while tonight. I gave myself my anniversary present, "shacking" soap and "sleeping" perfume.

Mrs. Miller asked me for Thanksgiving dinner. I had to refuse because I'm to dine with the Muntons. I was awakened tonight by a long distance call from San Francisco. Yes, it's my Irishman Jake. Just landed.

Saturday, November 20, 1943

Jake only weighs 145 lbs. He has a slight paralysis of the left leg. My poor dear boy.

It was a lovely day. What will life be like when Robert and I are separated? For him too, even more than I. The loneliness will be beyond words.

Monday, November 22, 1943

A British RAF flyer was killed in an auto accident last night. He was a Wing Commander. So very sad. The papers are full of talk about General George S. Patton Jr. dragging an American soldier out of a Sicilian hospital bed to make him fight. Col. Munton says Patton may have gone temporarily insane due to the strain of many campaigns.

When I mentioned that perhaps he should step down, Robert became incensed.

Wednesday, November 24, 1943

Tonight I got all dressed up for the Gladys Swarthout Concert. I wore my blue velvet blouse, black velvet skirt, blue fascinator and squirrel jacket.

Robert and I dined at Pierre's, all very elegant but no butter! C'est la querre! Swarthout was lovely. Her stage presence was outstanding. She wore a lovely green dress with a flowing skirt.

Thursday, November 25, 1943 Thanksgiving

Beautiful day, so crisp and cool out and just a dusting of snow. I had a marvelous dinner at the Munton's. We sat down about the same time we do at home, but of course it's nothing like home.

I had two helpings of turkey and trimmings. I never get a chance to have a home cooked meal, and I do so appreciate it. I feel as if I don't have to eat for a week. Mrs. Munton played the piano for us. Superb playing. She's really very talented. Six months after she married she was supposed to make her debut with the Philadelphia Orchestra. She had to give that dream up because of Col. Munton's career. As a military wife you have very little say over where you live. You can move at a moment's notice.

I am sleeping in Lily's room tonight. The canopy bed is so very cozy. It reminds me so much of my room at home.

Friday, November 26, 1943

We all got up early. I drove to the station with Robert and Mrs. Munton and then drove the car back through nerve wracking traffic to the Pentagon. There was not much doing for me at work so I took some more overtime. I got back to the Munton's and cleaned Lily's room up. I'm getting her ready for a dance tonight. It was reminiscent of old times when I went through the panic and furor of party preparations.

Saturday, November 27, 1943

I have a bad cold today. Can't stop sneezing and blowing. I went to town with the kids. I didn't want to disappoint them so we went to the movies tonight to see "The Gang's All Here." It was very funny and I enjoyed it thoroughly in spite of my cold.

We went for ice cream after the movie. We have such fun when we are together. Since it was Saturday night I thought it would be fun to play Society Craps. We didn't play with money of course. We found a jar of buttons in Mrs. Munton's sewing room. Carl emerged the victor.

Sunday, November 28, 1943

Stayed in all day. I prepared all three meals. We ate up the potatoes and dressing, but there is still some turkey left over. Jake called me today and asked if I would send him $50. He says he has spent $275 on me for Christmas. What am I going to do now? He also says the army is trying to give him a complete disability discharge. Naturally he doesn't want it.

I cooked fried tomatoes on bread for the kids. I asked Carl to set the table and promised him that we could play cards after dinner. Lily asked me to give her some tips on make-up. It sure is fun overseeing them.

Tuesday, November 30, 1943

I came to work. Robert had sent me a box of candy for the office, plus some rare postcards. I feel a lot better today. I got home and straightened everything up. Lily had too much home work so she didn't go to dinner with Carl and me at the Hot Shoppe. We drove down to the station to meet Robert and Mrs. Munton. How marvelous to see him again. How I missed him. There was a definite void.

Were there ever two people as much in love as we are? I doubt it. What will time do to us?

Monday, December 6, 1943

I bought a book of collected war stories for Robert for Christmas. I think it is just the right book for him. I have reservations on the train to Buffalo and return so there is nothing to worry about. I received two letters from Jake and he's still in the Brooke General Hospital at San Antonio.

I went to a swing concert by Duke Ellington. He performed C Jam Blue. It was really super. Kate went with me and we just couldn't sit still in our seats. That music just moves me so! We were so tired when we got home; we just plopped on the sofa.

I had a call from Jake when I got home. He seems to be much better and sounds like he is improving because he is very quick on the comeback. I'm very worried about this expensive gift he says he's giving me for Christmas. I don't think it would be right to accept it. A gift like that is most compromising. I'll have to write to him tonight and make that clear.

I wrote four lines of Sara Teasdale's poetry in the front of Robert's book before I went to bed. I think it describes Robert to perfection, and something even his wife could see.

Yet there is another poem of Teasdale's that I have written down and intend to give him before I leave on the train for Buffalo.

"I Am Not Yours"
I am not yours, not lost in you,
Not lost, although I long to be
Lost as a candle lit at noon,
Lost as a snowflake in the sea.
You love me, and I find you still
A spirit beautiful and bright,
Yet I am I, who long to be
Lost as a light is lost in light.
Oh plunge me deep in love -- put out
My senses, leave me deaf and blind,
Swept by the tempest of your love,
A taper in a rushing wind.

Sara Teasdale

Monday, December 13, 1943

Robert and I are up to our necks in work. The pressing subject is the joint assault signal company which is a "hot potato" if there ever was one. The abbreviation for this organization is "Jasco." I shall call my first dog by that name. I would like to have two dogs, so the other one would be called "Burp" of course.

Jake called. He has been moved from Brooke General Hospital to another place in San Antonio. He is feeling a lot better; he doesn't expect to get a furlough until after Christmas. He promised me that he is trying to put on some weight.

111

Robert and I dined at Pierre's tonight. I always feel very romantic sitting across from my love there. It seems as though it was from a script written just for us. The music is lovely; I have to remind myself to breathe. Then we went to a concert at the Constitution Hall. Darius Milhaud was supposed to be guest conductor, but he was ill, so Hans Kindler conducted. It was good tonight. They played "Scheherazade" by Rimsky-Korsakov. What a romantic thrill it was to hear this music that conveys the way we feel; such passion.

Thursday, December 16, 1943

I accompanied Robert to Lt. General DeWitt's office in the new War Dept. building. He was Perishing's Chief of Staff for S.O.S in the last war. The office was smooth. I talked with his aide while Robert was inside with General Dewitt.

I'm reading "The Prodigal Women" by Nancy Hale, very entertaining. Kate wants to read it next.

Saturday, December 18, 1943

Arrived at Army Ground Forces with Robert this morning just in time to see the trooping of the colors. The band was playing the "Dashing White Sergeant." There is such a swell of excitement that you feel when you hear the band play. It's almost impossible to keep your emotions intact.

I wrote to mother when I got home. I'm so looking forward to Christmas, the lights, the bustling on Buffalo City streets. Oh, and the delicious food. It's funny how small Buffalo seems to me now. I know they say you can never go home again. And I understand that sentiment, but isn't home simply the place where you are loved the most? Right now I don't know where that would be.

Robert told me he knows the date and location of the next allied blow, or offensive rather, at the axis. This is a very powerful man. I must not allow myself to cause him any distractions. He needs my strength, not my whimpering.

Friday, December 24, 1943

A full day Christmas party at the office. A wild dash to the florist to pick up an orchid Robert ordered for me. Traffic was terrible. I almost didn't get there in time. Robert put me on the train and I made him open his presents in the berth. He loves all I gave him, especially the four lines of poetry I wrote in the book, "Men at War."

The train was three hours late getting into Buffalo. I had a grand time talking to some Canadian air forces girls in the ladies room. I didn't sleep a wink last night as usual. Wonderful to see Mother and Dad. We went for cocktails at the Myer's. Dad works with Mr. Myer. I met their son Stuart, very smooth. You could tell both sets of parents were making wedding plans for us in their minds.

Before I went to bed I placed my presents under the adorable little table top tree. Lovely sight.

Saturday, December 25, 1943

Mother and Dad were delirious over my gifts. Mother said I always know just what to get for them. I received some beautiful presents, loads of perfume and a new dress. It was like old times visiting all of the neighbors, then off to Aunt Millie's. It was grand seeing Carol and Laura.

Jake called from New York. He got to his sisters today.

Our table looked elegant and cocktails and dinner were out of this world. Stuart came over tonight. We went to the Statler Bar. Mother and Dad looked very pleased with themselves.

Monday, December 27, 1943

The train miraculously was only a half hour late. Robert met me. Perfect being with him again. The office was all agog over the fun gifts I brought back for them.

Robert gave me his gifts in his private office. They are so beautiful I can hardly believe they are mine. One is a black reptile bag fitted with Elizabeth Arden compact, lipstick, silver match box, comb and place for cigarettes. The other is a real satin blue nightgown trimmed with Italian lace and a matching chiffon negligee with lace. Truly a trousseau piece. When I was a little girl I dreamed of things like this. I never thought it could happen to me.

I met Jake on the 7:30 train. He doesn't look too bad. Still the same fascinating Irishman. He is staying here at Mrs. Nelson's.

Friday, December 31, 1943

Jake and I spent a quiet New Year's Eve with Kate and Mrs. Nelson. Mrs. Nelson sprang for two bottles of champagne in honor of Jake's safe return. It was snowing softly outside. Robert told me not to expect a Happy New Year phone call, as he and Mrs. Munton were celebrating with friends; much like last year.

Jake has his old room back and Kate is back in with me. I don't mind. Robert hasn't been "dropping by" lately because of all of the work we are doing. After Kate went to bed I met Jake in the living room. Mrs. Nelson had retired early. Jake told me all about his adventures. His leg was hurt in a plane crash and he was almost burned from high octane gas. While he was in the hospital they took too much fluid from his spine and he was "out" for two days and woke up with terrible pain. He watched the Japs bomb a China village from a slit trench and went through the village after. It's all true what they say. He flew a lot, evacuating Chinese women and children and missionaries from Burma. He truly is a hero.

When he finished talking he looked at me kind of queer, then he said let's get out of here and celebrate! We went to the 400 Club, and it was $2.00 per person cover charge just for sitting at a table. He said he didn't care one bit; it was worth it to celebrate the New Year with me. He bought a bottle of champagne and some lobster cakes for the table. At the stroke of midnight he took me in his arms and kissed me. He kissed me like he never had before.

This was my year for Love.

Saturday, January 1, 1944

Worked all day as usual. Colonel Munton felt badly about asking me to work tonight as well. The work is too important to ever think of saying no. Jake is angry that I have to work so much. He is so possessive. He wants me to do everything that he wants. It must stop. He must realize I am a free and independent being, living a life of my own.

Sunday, January 2, 1944

Jake and I took a long walk after breakfast. I worked until a quarter to nine. We had a long talk. He is desperately in love, and that is all there is to it.

I tried to explain to him just how I feel. It is no easy job.

Tuesday, January 4, 1944

Robert and I came up to New York City tonight for a conference to be held tomorrow at the Bell Laboratories. We are staying at the Astor. It is smooth. We had scotch highballs in the Columbia Room, it's dripping with elegance. I feel like quite the lady. It is after midnight and I hope I get a good night's sleep so I can be fit for tomorrow.

Thursday, January 6, 1944

After work Jake and I went shopping. I had to return Mother's gloves, they didn't fit her correctly. Poor Jake looked longingly at all the civilian clothes. Jake and I had dinner with Kate at Pierre's; he held the floor naturally, talking about India. We came back to our room and talked for three hours. He wants to get the experience in India out of his mind. I'm glad I'm here to listen. I guess it is hard answering everyone's questions.

I love looking into those beautiful hazel eyes and brushing his soft brown hair back with my fingers. How adorable Jake is. The Irish are certainly a lovable and devastatingly attractive people.

116

Friday, January 7, 1944

Robert and I had dinner at Evan's Coffee Shoppe. We stopped at a drug store around the corner which has a fine collection of perfumes. Robert bought me Lanvin "Scandal." You can't buy it any more at department stores so I consider myself very lucky.

I just noticed, Robert's hairline is beginning to recede.

Saturday, January 8, 1944

I had dinner with Robert. Jake was very mad. In fact he had his bag packed to leave. He is so jealous. I really can't blame him though. A man in love is like that. He cooled down however, and we saw a swell thrilling show, "Destination Tokyo," when I got back.

Sunday, January 9, 1944

Robert and I had a long talk instead of working. I cried a great deal. Everything seems so mixed up.

I even confided that I care for Jake a great deal. He guided me to a clearer understanding of that relationship. Oh to have someone who understands you so completely. We two had a grand talk on sex, marriage, ideals etc.

Monday, January 10, 1944

I had lunch with Jake today. I introduced him to some of the kids in the office. For the first time I noticed how nervous he is. It will take some time for him to get back to normal. Having escaped with your life about three times doesn't leave one exactly calm. He flew to New York today to see his sister. From there he'll go to the Rest Camp in Atlantic City.

I am so tired tonight. This is the culmination of a very hectic emotional life.

117

Tuesday, January 11, 1944

Jake called me at the office from his sisters. No news, but misses me terribly. I can't help being in love with him a little. He's very handsome and kind. He has great integrity as well. You can't help loving someone when they love you so much. He is a dear sweet boy, and I wish he would make something wonderful of himself for me. I have confidence in him and know that he could reach great heights. Then I would seriously consider marrying him.

I received a letter from Aunt Millie today. She sent me a lock of Dad's baby hair - a treasure of Grammie's.

Thursday, January 13, 1944

I did all my chores tonight. Dusted my room, washed and ironed and played Society Craps with Kate and a friend of hers, Lizzy. It's funny how people can resemble their names. Lizzy seems a little dizzy. I only won 24 cents tonight.

Robert came over rather late and was annoyed that I was with my friends. He wanted to talk with me. We went for a ride and he took off on this rampage. He said he has always been, and probably always will be the old reliable type, not dangerous like Jake and others. It's true I guess, but its Robert's type that always wins out in the end.

Friday, January 14, 1944

Jake called this morning from Atlantic City. He asked me to wire him fifty dollars. His brother got in some sort of scrape I guess. He said he'd write me the details.

Went over to Ground Forces with Col. Munton. Everyone is so friendly over there. And do those girls ever envy me my job. I know just how lucky I am.

There's one girl whom Col. Munton calls "Honey Child", she just worships him. Do I blame her? I should say not.

Saturday, January 15, 1944

It is snowing tonight for the first time this month. It reminds me of Buffalo. Jake called from Atlantic City. I swear his voice over the phone gets me. He says words cannot be spoken of how much he misses me. I wish he were the "Golden Knight" but fear he never will be.

Sunday, January 16, 1944

Gorgeous day - the world is decked in white. Robert and I took a walk around the Pentagon. It was so beautiful it almost hurt. A lot of planes flew over us. My heart lifts every time.

Tuesday, January 18, 1944

Today was the first session of the airborne conference. It was quite interesting. I took practically everything down verbatim.

I had dinner with the Muntons. Robert and I came back and worked until 12:30, I was really dead, but I loved it.

On top of everything else, I forgot my keys and didn't discover it until we got all the way home. Had to go back to the Pentagon for them.

Wednesday, January 19, 1944

Tonight was Yehudi Menuhin's concert at Constitution Hall. I was terribly disappointed. His selections were purely to show off his technique, no melody at all. The redeeming feature of the evening was that I saw the movie actress Madeleine Carroll in her Red Cross uniform. She is a very beautiful woman, and so inspiring for our troops.

I received a call from Jake tonight from Atlantic City. He is so darned possessive it irks me. Dealing with a jealous Irishman is nothing simple.

Friday, January 21, 1944

Mrs. Munton and Lily are going to New York for the weekend and Col. Munton is going to Fort Monmouth tomorrow, and I am going to take care of Carl.

I went home with them tonight. I washed all my undies in the kitchen sink. Sure felt swell to be able to soak all the clothes at once. Being in a house every once in a while gives me a nostalgic feeling for home.

Saturday, January 22, 1944

Carl and I went to the Hot Shoppe for dinner and then to the movies, he's such a sweet kid. Carl asked if we could play Society Craps before his dad got home. I made a fire and some hot chocolate. They have those old fashioned popcorn grates that you can shake over the fire. That was great fun. Col. Munton came home and joined in. Mrs. Munton doesn't approve of her children playing Society Craps. She feels it's inappropriate and not a wholesome game to encourage. It will be our little secret.

Monday, January 24, 1944

We have a new maid here at Mrs. Nelson's who is truly super. Our room is immaculate and inspires neatness in its occupants. She even dusts my bureau with its multitude of bottles of perfume and lotions.

Every once in a while I like to record how dearly I love Robert. What a miracle that he should love me and he thinks it is a miracle that I love him. I do not particularly like to dwell on the future. In fact I avoid it as much as possible.

Saturday, January 29, 1944

Jake is in town for the weekend. He looks fine. We went to the movies and saw a perfectly swell show, a war time picture and I got excited as usual. After the show Jake and I walked down Rock Creek

Drive, Constitution Avenue and then back home. It must have been five miles, it was a lovely night. We didn't really talk very much. It was just nice being together. He went back to Atlantic City at 8:00 p.m. Kate is back in his room again.

I bought a cute Valentine to send to Carl. I think he has a little crush on me. Like father, like son!

Tuesday, February 1, 1944

Worked tonight for a couple of hours. It is endless. There is so little time to really sit down and think about all that is going on these days. My job is so interesting and I come in contact with so many fascinating people that I do wish I could memorize or record my observations of the administration of this war. I cannot forget the sights that thrill either; planes flying over the Pentagon, the trooping of the colors every Saturday morning at the Army War College and many others.

Friday, February 4, 1944

Jake called. Wish he would use his persistence in the proper direction, like getting ahead in the army. He said he's coming in early tomorrow.

I'm really thinking it's time that I get an apartment of my own. Kate is talking about moving home. My job takes me away from the house so much, and Mrs. Nelson is still a little odd. I don't understand why she doesn't want to take in any new boarders. Her paranoia is so unwarranted. She wasn't at all like this when we first moved in. War affects people in so many different and strange ways. Some people become stronger and some become weaker. I'm certainly not the same naïve girl I was when I first got off the train such a short time ago, yet so long ago.

Saturday, February 5, 1944

Jake came in. He brought me a lovely blue Chatlaw blanket he won at a Red Cross bingo party. I called Mother up tonight and she said it was all right to accept the blanket. We saw "The Uninvited" with Ray Milland and a new young actress. I can't remember her name. It was so haunting, but beautiful. It was set on the Irish Sea with a little town down the road. Wouldn't it be wonderful if Robert and I could have a little cottage of our own? I wouldn't want to dream of a grand mansion like in "Rebecca", just a lovely little cottage with a garden and our dogs, Jasco and Burp. We could get up in the morning and go in to town for our paper and coffee. At night we would sit out after dinner with Jasco by our feet and watch the waves roll in. I shouldn't even think of it.

Sunday, February 6, 1944

Jake and I had a luxurious breakfast at the Mayflower dining room. He wanted to splurge and do something totally out of the ordinary. We lingered a little over our coffee and people watched for a while. There were so many soldiers and their sweethearts walking in and out of the lobby. How sweet.

Robert took me to hear Albert Spaulding, the renowned violinist. I wore my pink chiffon dress with the matching cape. I do hope I wasn't over dressed for a Sunday afternoon. Robert said that I looked like an angel, and that was good enough for me.

I was completely mesmerized throughout. He played the Elgar concerto and I have yet to recover.

My days are so beautifully full.

Thursday, February 10, 1944

Good news! Kate's sister Linda is coming to stay at the house. Mrs. Nelson was very gracious and inviting. Knowing that it's Kate's sister, and that she comes from a good home, puts her mind at ease. I think Mrs. Nelson is better because she has been given some nerve pills by her doctor. She really is ever so much more relaxed. I was so worried about Kate leaving. I really didn't want to be living in the house alone with Mrs. Nelson. The two sisters are going to have the larger room and I will keep the smaller downstairs room. I believe Linda will be moving in close to St. Patrick's Day.

Jake sent me six lovely flowered hankies for Valentine's Day. He's so thoughtful and darling.

Col. Munton took me to dinner. I had to get very bundled up, the weather is so cold. Strong gale blowing temperature down to 15 degrees F.

Saturday, February 13, 1944

I wrote to Mother and Dad. I have so little time to catch up on my correspondence. If I were in battle I couldn't spend any time on writing letters.

Robert and I talked mostly all day. We didn't get much work done.

Jake called tonight. He has made some momentous decision regarding us and we are to talk it over when he sees me.

Monday, February 14, 1944

Robert and I went to The Watergate Inn for dinner and then to the movies. It was a riot, it was all about Washington. It was called, "Standing Room Only." Robert gave me a new perfume called "Moroccan Rose" for Valentine's Day. It is in a very unusual box.

I got home to find a gorgeous card from Jake. It has a picture of a garden with a real red satin frame. The verse inside is a lovely sentiment. I know I shall keep it always. Jake called, says he's all mixed up.

Tuesday, February 15, 1944

In the space of one instant I saw Admiral Leahy and General Marshall over in the Combined Chiefs of Staff Building. I didn't know General Marshall, I wasn't looking at him but he brushed my arm coming up the stairs. How thrilling.

Jake called. He is leaving for Patterson Field Ohio early tomorrow morning. He expects eventually to be with his commanding officer, Col. Garlock.

The work pace is nothing short of terrific. I feel I'm in a whirl these days, personally and professionally. Robert's efforts are unwavering. Men like him are winning this war. He is so adorable. Our day of separation will bring to me the full realization of my love for him.

I'm reading a new book, "The Man in Grey" by Lady Eleanor Smith.

Wednesday, February 23, 1944

Robert and I attended a marvelous concert tonight. Ezio Pinza was guest star. His voice is excellent and he drew a great deal of applause. The highlight of the program for me however was the "Romeo & Juliet Overture," it never fails to thrill me.

Tragic love stories are so haunting. I do so hope that our love story will have a happy ending.

I was thinking of getting a new hair style and I passed the idea by Robert. He said he loves the way my hair looks and doesn't want me to change one strand. He certainly has strong opinions.

Friday, February 25th, 1944

Jake wrote from Patterson Field asking me to loan him $50. I am not sending it. I haven't the extra cash, and I will not touch my savings account. My income tax is $107.94. It's a wonderful feeling to realize I have the money to pay it.

I went to the movies with Col. Munton and Carl tonight. We saw Joan Fontaine and Orson Wells in "Jane Eyre." It was just like the book, very somber, but fascinating all the same. Fontaine was perfection as Jane Eyre. You could feel her heart aching. The part when the wife is screaming up in the tower made poor little Carl curl up in his seat. Col. Munton stared straight ahead at the screen. I put my arm around Carl to comfort him.

When Carl and I went up to the concession stand for popcorn he thanked me for the Valentine. He's such a sweet kid.

Friday, March 3, 1944

Jake sent me an Army Air Forces sweetheart scarf. It is darling. That boy can think of more ways to spend money, and let me know that he loves me.

I finished reading "The Marshall" by Mary Raymond Shipman Andrews. It is an exquisite, romantic story, but oh so sad an ending. It is one of Robert's favorite books. The date inside the cover is 1916.

How very fortunate I am to be able to work every day with the man that I love during the greatest war in history so far. Side by side we are accomplishing so much.

Monday, March 6, 1944

Worked late tonight. When we came out it was pouring rain and we had to run to the car. It struck me all of a sudden, this is the life. There is no excuse for those blue spells of mine.

I came home and soaked myself in a hot tub with pine bath oil. Feels delicious. Almost worth being caught in the rain.

Wednesday, March 8, 1944

Went to the concert with dear Robert, heard Kabelevsky's 2nd Symphony which impressed me so much. I'm convinced the Russians are the best composers by far. Many years from now I will remember these concerts, sitting beside Robert with my hand in his. When the music is particularly beautiful we always turn and look at each other.

Thursday, March 9, 1944

Stuart Myer, the young man I met at home over Christmas, was in town. He asked me to join him for dinner. Went dining and dancing at the Victory Room of the Roosevelt Hotel. The orchestra there is grand and there were just a handful of people dancing, almost unheard of in Washington. Stuart likes his work very much at his law firm in Buffalo. His goal is to make partner someday.

Mother has hinted to me that Stuart would make a fine husband. He and his family belong to The Saturn Club of Buffalo.

She said a young man like that won't remain on the market for long. She can't really expect me to move back to Buffalo at this point. And my work here is so vital. Robert says that I do the work of three stenographers. I simply couldn't move home.

Friday, March 10, 1944

I worked with Robert three hours overtime tonight working on the diagrams. They really get me. I am so tired. He says I'm too tense.

I got a very brusque note from Jake. He evidently intends to ignore my last letter which roasted him a plenty for complaining so much about the army.

Tuesday, March 14, 1944

Jake is not coming back to Washington because he has been ordered overseas. Why did that happen out of the blue?

The Pope is pleading for Rome to be spared, just a voice crying in the wilderness.

I will be praying tonight for my dear Jake and for Rome.

We all must pray for our soldiers who are fighting every day and risking their lives. So many brave young men.

Wednesday, March 15, 1944

It was just like spring today. Temperature went up to 79 degrees. I think it is sort of a freak spell.

Got Jakes laundry mailed at last. I hope I don't have to bother with it anymore, it's quite an imposition and Jake doesn't seem to realize it.

I went to the movies with Robert tonight. He is adorable. He is so like a little boy and he does have a look of innocence in those blue eyes. He needs me so much. I wonder how long it will be before he is ordered to the field or overseas. They are all going, one by one.

How will I be able to go on with Jake gone, and at some point Robert will be sent away as well. Tomorrow is St. Patrick's Day. I always think of Jake on St. Patrick's Day. I'll be humming "When Irish Eyes are Smiling" all day long I'm sure.

Mrs. Nelson is doing much better these days. I truly feel her nerve pills have helped a great deal. She doesn't have the old spark of life she once had. I wish there was something I could do to help her. She does like it when I go to church with her. I'm going to have to try to make the effort.

Friday, March 17, 1944

Today being St. Patrick's Day I really dressed for the occasion; green sweater, green coat, green hat and gloves and green umbrella too. I was invited over to Mrs. Miller's for dinner tonight for corned beef and cabbage. She makes boiled carrots and potatoes and there will, I hope, be sour cream on the side. That's what she usually does when she makes it.

Monday, March 20, 1944

I talked with a major just back from Italy. He says it's terribly dirty over there but the Italians are very nice and hospitable, but oh so hungry. They scrape the mess plates of the soldiers.

Kate and Linda met me for lunch at the Mayflower Hotel today. Since Robert pays for most of my meals I have been able to save quite a bit. I thought I would treat them, as they could never afford to go there. Linda is darling, only eighteen and she's looking for a job.

I used my new reptile bag that Robert gave me for Christmas. I didn't want to use it when it was so cold and wet out. Kate admired it; I had to tell her I bought it myself. I guessed at the price, $40.00 I said. I wish I could say Robert had given it to me, but alas there are things one cannot tell.

It was just two years ago today that I came to Washington.

Wednesday, March 22, 1944

Robert and I went to Pierre's for dinner. Then to the concert. Tonight was the last one of the Wednesday night subscription concerts and it was the best. Josef Hoffman, probably the world's greatest pianist, was the soloist. His playing was sublime. I had thought I knew what good piano playing was, but I guess I was wrong. He played the concerto No. 2 in F Minor by Chopin.

Thursday, March 23, 1944

The Japs have pushed into India at the Burma border, but have been cut off already. The fighting around Cassino in Italy is fierce.

I wrote to Mother and Dad tonight. I miss them. I was supposed to have started menstruating today, but no sign of anything.

Saturday, March 25, 1944

Went up to Maureen's to stay all night. She had rum cakes and a grand dinner awaiting me. We ate by candlelight. Her apartment is darling. She has matching bookcases with a writing desk in between. Her eye for color is impeccable, soft blues, not deep. It's just a one bedroom with an intimate dining nook, a very small, but functional, kitchen and an area for entertaining. There was a photo of her husband in one of the open bookcases. My, but is he a looker. We talked about everything worthwhile, nothing too deeply personal. I could never tell her about Robert and me. Someday, perhaps, but not any time soon.

Sunday, March 26, 1944

Beautiful spring day. Maureen and I drove out in Maryland to a celebrated eating place, Mrs. K's Toll House Tavern, delicious food. Maureen became a little misty eyed for no reason at all. When I asked her what was wrong, she said she hadn't been back to this particular spot since her husband left. They used to come here all the time. I can certainly understand how she must feel. I don't even want to think about what I will go through the first time I go to the Watergate Inn when, and if, Robert is sent away.

Monday, March 27, 1944

I had cramps all day. Felt so awful I couldn't record a conference. Lucky that Maureen could take over for me.

Robert and I watched a lovely sunset tonight. It is such a comfort to be with him when I feel bad. He is a very soothing person, my darling is.

I got a letter from Jake. He is in a better frame of mind than before.

I feel awful. I'm going to take a bath and go to bed.

Wednesday, March 29, 1944

I had a few cramps today. I guess I am having such a bad time because I was late this month; very relieved though.

Robert and I worked for a couple of hours tonight. He seemed preoccupied and short with me.

Friday, March 31, 1944

My work has definitely been slipping of late. I am absolutely the most security conscious employee in the War Department. How could I have left the safe combination lying on top of our safe this evening? I didn't tell Col. Munton. He'd have a fit. I have resolved to be more careful about my work. Col. Munton is going to bawl me out furiously if I do anything wrong.

I should start knitting something. Following a pattern always helps me to get my mind back on track.

Monday, April 3, 1944

All cafés and restaurants here are cutting down the variety on menus due to shortage of help.

Kleenex is scarce, but I manage to keep ahead of the game. Mother sends me some in the laundry box. Col. Munton gets me some at the PX, and Col. Harrison got me two boxes the other day when they were being unpacked at the drug store in the Pentagon.

It snowed late this afternoon. Seemed odd to see a white blanket on the pink cherry blossom buds. I hope the blossoms will be able to survive. A nice day of sun should bring them back to life again, I hope.

I do like Major David, the British Secretary of the Recognition Committee, extremely well. He always smiles at me several times during meetings, and of course I smile back.

The U.S. destroyed all Japanese ships at three naval bases in the Pacific.

I got a pink hat tonight, but it doesn't match the collar or cuffs on my coat. It was only $3.98 however.

Got a letter from Jake.

I can't wait for the snow to be gone.

Wednesday, April 5, 1944

Soon we will be finishing the revision of the joint amphibious communications. It will then be expedited to all theaters. Robert is well known for his expert advice on amphibious matters. He receives letters from all theaters regularly.

I worked a couple of extra hours tonight. I know that never again will I enjoy working as much as I do now. I must get all I can out of this. In life you must take everything as it comes. I'm trying so hard to learn this.

Worries over, I got a darling pink straw hat which matches my pink collar and cuffs exactly. I intend to get some blue veiling for it.

Saturday, April 8, 1944

I stayed after hours tonight and wrote to Mother and Dad and Jake. Kate and Linda and I are going to go to the sunrise service tomorrow at Arlington Cemetery. The Marine Band will play, and General Marshall is going to offer a prayer for the Armed Forces, and put the Cross of Lilies on the Tomb of the Unknown Soldier.

Sunday, April 9, 1944

I got up at 5:30 a.m. A lovely day. Sunrise service was beautiful, 10,000 people attended. This was one of the loveliest Easter Sunday's of my life. I should say the loveliest so far. I'm so glad that I went. I might never again have the opportunity. More people turned out for church and the cherry blossoms; there were more than any other year in Washington's history. I saw Mrs. Nelson with some of her friends from church. She had a grand smile on her face.

There was such a sense of community and strength, it was palpable.

Friday, April 14, 1944

I went over to the Army War College. A lovelier spot could never be found at this time of year. The cherry blossoms and forsythia bushes are out in such glory.

I am literally walking on air. I bought a beautiful navy blue twill suit at a new store in town. It has a cardigan that matches, I just couldn't resist, and it all fits perfectly. I wanted something new for Mother and Dad's visit. It only took those two years to get here, but I am not going to complain.

I received a letter from Dad tonight saying they will arrive at 5:35 p.m. Tuesday. I'm going to call them this weekend and try to persuade them to take an earlier train.

I worked so fast and furiously today I didn't take time to eat until 3:00. I am so happy. I said to Robert that life is so wonderful sometimes you wish you could remember each detail of the particular time, so you could live it again accurately in memory. Then he gave me a sweet smile.

My suit was ready thank goodness! Robert gave me a preliminary birthday gift which I am very pleased with, a bottle of "Cobra" perfume. He says it's deadly like I am.

Tuesday, April 18, 1944

It was hard to concentrate all day, especially at the conference this afternoon. Finally it was time to taxi to the station. Mother looked perfectly stunning in a gray gabardine Rosenblum suit with violet blouse and matching hat. Dad had on a new topcoat and brown Homburg hat.

We went for cocktails at The Annapolis. Harry, the bartender there makes the very best martini, Mother and Dad's favorite. After cocktails we went to the Watergate Inn for dinner. After we dined we walked to the Lincoln Memorial which they were thrilled with. They gave me a Parker pen and pencil set for my birthday, three pairs of stockings, and a lovely summer green suit with a green and white candy striped blouse.

Wednesday, April 19, 1944

I didn't take off at all today. However, Mother and Dad really got around;, the Capital, Supreme Court, Folger Shakespeare Library, and the National Gallery of Art, as well as Mellon Art Gallery. Tonight we had dinner at the Annapolis where they are staying, and then we went to the Congressional Library.

The head man took us on a tour and we went all over, down in the sub-basement even. He showed us how the books are sent over to Congress in huge tubes. I can feel how thrilled they are to be here. I love how their faces light up when they see something they have never seen before.

Thursday, April 20, 1944

Today was quite a nice day. Mother and Dad came over to the Pentagon, I introduced them to everybody. We went to lunch at the Little Tea House with Col. Munton. Mother and Dad are crazy about him as I knew they would be. We then went to Mt. Vernon in Col. Munton's Buick. Mother and Dad loved it. Truly it is gorgeous with all the trees in bloom. There are some beautiful purple blossoms which surpass the cherry blossoms.

I know this might sound strange, but I find Mt. Vernon very romantic. Every young couple should come here while they are deeply in love, not encumbered with the troubles that marriage can sometimes bring.

Tonight I took Mother and Dad to Pierre's for dinner. They said they had never before eaten such marvelous food. It was so much like old times sitting and sharing a meal with my parents. I do miss them so.

Friday, April 21, 1944

Mother and Dad and I went to luncheon with Col. Munton and Mrs. Munton at the Watergate Inn. We had a grand time. It was a nice day. I showed them Jefferson Memorial and the pansy beds which are in full bloom. The cherry blossoms are out completely and are simply gorgeous.

We had an excellent fish dinner at O'Donnell's. Mother said she hopes she hasn't gained a great deal of weight on this trip, but the food was too delicious for words.

Mother and Dad took the 8:15 home to Buffalo. It was so sad saying goodbye to them. They are so dear and we had such a grand time. Well, back to work I guess.

Tuesday, April 25, 1944

I received a letter from Jake yesterday. He says he has been trying to forget me, but no go. He loves me more than ever.

I went to bed at 9:15 last night so of course I felt loads better today, but yet, not quite up to par. I miss Mother and Dad terribly. Having them here was such a treat. At least they were here when the weather was grand. It's rather cool today. I hope they will come and visit me again soon. Now that they know how much there is to do here I'm sure that they will.

Thursday, April 27, 1944

"Joint Amphibian Communication" went to the General's office this morning. It's in great need by our forces. Big operations in the future will use it, perhaps the invasion forces in Europe.

How dearly I love Robert. He is so much a part of me. How will I face life without him some day? They say a human being can surmount to anything everything and I hope I won't prove an exception.

Tuesday, May 2, 1944

I received an unexpected windfall in the mail. New York State has refunded $5.89 to me for not deducting 25% from my tax return.

The weather continues to be lovely. The dogwood trees are in full bloom. The landscaping around the Pentagon is beautiful now. In a few years it will be a showplace.

My interest in politics is reviving with the campaign war at hand. It looks like Dewey will be the Republican nominee. I feel sorry for the President. He has aged so from his responsibilities. There really is no one who can fill his shoes on the Democratic side.

Work tonight. Endless!

Saturday, May 6, 1944

I got up early and went over to the Munton's to rake leaves in their yard. It was good exercise and fun to be with the kids.

Mrs. Munton had a grand meal ready for us; baked beans, potato salad, sliced ham and cheese, sandwich rolls, olives and apricot jam.

Monday, May 8, 1944

The office force are all making bets on when the invasion will be. I haven't made a choice as yet. It's all guesswork.

Worked late tonight. A blackout interrupted everything and it lasted an hour. The Pentagon would have been like a tomb if it hadn't been for the air conditioning noise. It was so quiet and frightening I could almost hear my own heart beating. What would I have done without Robert by my side?

Tuesday, May 9, 1944

We received word today that "Joint Amphibian Communications" has been approved by the Joint Communications Board. We are all thrilled. No changes were made in it except adding U.S. to the title. Tonight Col. Munton took all of us in the office to the Watergate Inn for dinner. We had super cocktails, and what a steak dinner, perfect! And we had plum cream for dessert.

I wrote to Jake tonight. I just started thinking about him and I wanted to see how he is doing. I don't know how close he is to his sister, but he not having a mother just breaks my heart. I want him to know that there is someone out there who cares about him.

I'm going to make a pair of socks for Jake. If that works out I could knit him a sweater for Christmas. I'm not sure how long that would take. Jackie knows how to knit; I think I'll ask her to find an easy pattern for me. I'm always amazed at how she will take her knitting bag with her to the movies and work on something through the entire movie.

Thursday, May 18, 1944

We were going to work tonight, but Col. Munton decided we would go to the movies and relax. We picked up the family and saw "Cover Girl." Very good. Carl will soon be twelve. He's grown so much in the last two years. He is crazy about me and reminisces about the good times we have had together. He is adorable. I am very fond of him.

Sunday, May 21, 1944

Col. Munton took me shopping in Clarendon. I bought two rayon nighties, a Father's Day card, a birthday card for Maureen, and a graduation card for my cousin Laura. I can't believe she is graduating from high school.

I expected to work all day but a nice surprise happened. Lt. Jeffers and Col. Argus came over and we all went out to dinner with the Muntons and then went to the movies.

Col. Argus asked me to dance several times. I could tell that Robert wanted to cut in, but he dared not.

Monday, May 22, 1944

I got a letter from Jake. He has received my Christmas package which I mailed to India last October. It has been all around the world. I think that is wonderful that nothing has happened to it.

Robert is adorable. I love him dearly. He claims I will meet someone someday finer than he is. I don't see how I can, but stranger things have happened. I have a feeling that this is the last summer Robert and I will be together. If I could only face the future unafraid. Robert reasons with me and is very patient, but I guess you just can't get anything across to a woman along those lines.

Saturday, May 27, 1944

War News:

The U.S. Fifth & Eighth armies have joined and are pushing up the Italian peninsula. They are now 18 miles from Rome to which the Germans are fleeing. Maybe the invasion will start any day now, striking while the iron is hot.

Robert and I went to see Charles Boyer and Ingrid Bergman in "Gaslight." It was spell binding and I sat on the edge of my seat most of the time. I loved the plot about an unscrupulous cad played by Boyer. He was so devilish in the role. Bergman was delicate, yet so fierce at the end. Joseph Cotton was also in the picture and I have decided he is one of my favorites. It was so thrilling the way came in and saved her at the end.

Wednesday, May 31, 1944

I received a letter from Jake. He doesn't like Patterson Field. I don't think he ever will be satisfied. He's dying to get back to Washington.

The allies are nearing Rome. Invasion of Europe should come soon. All America is waiting. What a day that will be!

Friday, June 2, 1944

I worked an hour tonight then came home to pack my suitcase. I'm to stay at the Munton's for three days to play "momma." Mrs. Munton is going to see her godson's graduation at West Point.

I'll have to plan some fun activities for the children. Once, I thought of being a teacher. I may have if the war didn't happen. Who knows what anyone of us would have become if the war didn't happen.

Saturday, June 3, 1944

Col. Munton and I met Lily and Carl in Clarendon. They took a taxi in and you could tell that they felt rather grand having done so.

We went to Fort Myer Commissary, had dinner at the Gray Stone Inn and then looked around the town. I got a darling two piece bathing suit at Garfunkel's. I tried several on for Robert to help me choose while the kids had ice cream across the street.

Sunday, June 4, 1944

War News:

The American 5th & 8th armies under General Clark captured Rome today. Nazis are in full retreat. Cold weather today.

Monday, June 5, 1944

The papers say entering Rome was like a carnival. Italians jubilant and rained confetti on our men.

It's grand having a spree at the Munton's. My bed is so comfortable here.

Tuesday, June 6, 1944

D-Day is here!

At 12:30 this a.m. the first flash came from the German radio. The allies have secured two beachheads. 11,000 planes, 4000 ships and thousands of smaller craft made up the greatest invasion armada in history.

Col. Mitchell, one of our breakfast club members, knew in advance of the invasion and was at the Pentagon all night.

The president will have the nation in prayer tonight.

Wednesday, June 7, 1944

The invasion is going better than expected and casualties are light. One percent loss of aircraft the first day. Churches all over the nation are filled with worshippers. A German counter attack is anticipated soon. Our forces in Italy are beyond Rome and have crossed the Tiber River.

I had one of my blue spells yesterday and Robert is in torture. I must overcome this great unease of mine or I shall be subject to unnecessary unhappiness for the rest of my life.

Thursday, June 8, 1944

The allies are twenty miles inland in France. I thought of Maureen today. She must be wondering if her husband is a part of the invasion. No way to tell for quite a while.

Yesterday was the junior high prom. Lily looked lovely in her pink dress. I helped her and her friend get ready.

Monday, June 12, 1944

Maureen and I had dinner at the Hot Shoppe and then talked in a lovely spot at the Pentagon river entrance. Col .Condon happened to be working late and said he'd take us home. Instead we went back to his bachelor pad apartment for a scotch and soda. We had such an interesting evening. He is a graduate of the Naval Academy. He's been all over the world, has met Clarence Darrow and knows a lot of interesting facts about pre-Pearl Harbor days in the navy. He is so shy. Wonder if he'd be daring enough to ask a girl out?

Tuesday, June 13, 1944

All the talk is that the war in Germany will be over this year, maybe. The war in China however is not going well. The Japs are making some waves that will prolong the Pacific war.

Friday, June 16, 1944

I had a letter from Jake last night. He is now in Indianapolis assisting WAC recruiting into the air transport command. He sent a clipping showing his picture and telling all about his adventures in India, real publicity. The first paragraph really sings his praises:

"As a warning to all Indianapolis short-snorters*, let it be known that the champion has arrived in town. He is Corporal Jake T.

O'Malley, 25-year-old veteran of the Air Transport Command who has completed 20 round trips "over the hump" of the Himalaya Mountains in Asia.

He has collected a short-snorter bill from almost every country he's visited during his 10 months of foreign duty and if the bills were pasted end to end they would make a strip 15 feet long."

*A short-snorter is a banknote which was signed by various persons traveling together, or meeting up at different events and records who was met. The tradition was started by bush pilots in Alaska in the 1920's, and subsequently spread through the growth of military and commercial aviation. If you signed a short-snorter and that person could not produce it upon request, they owed you a dollar, or a drink (a "short-snort", aviation and alcohol do not mix!)

Saturday, June 17, 1944

Insufferable heat. I waited twenty minutes for a bus to go out to Mrs. Millers. I got there alive but her apartment was unbearable. I had some Cuba Libres (rum, coke and lime) which helped a little. She handed out fans that a friend sent to her from China. The more I fanned myself the hotter I got.

Finally I asked if I could take a cool tub. She was such a darling. She lent me a robe and we lounged outside until a cool breeze came. Lovely.

Sunday, June 18, 1944

Jake called me at the office. He was so enthusiastic over his new assignment. He says he was picked for the job. I'm proud of him. I'm pleased to see him taking initiative and pride in his work.

I wonder if his enthusiasm has anything to do with being surrounded by young lonely women. It is a strange feeling thinking of him being interested in another woman. I took his heart out tonight and held it tight in my hand. I don't know what to think.

Tuesday, June 20, 1944

War News:

The allies have isolated the Cherbourg Peninsula from the Germans. They are almost at Cherbourg.

It was lovely and cool all day. I did all my ironing and changed the position of the furniture in my room when I got home from work. I am deeply engrossed in "Raleigh's Eden" by Inglis Clark Fletcher.

There is a big naval battle looming in the Pacific with major units of the Jap fleet.

The weather continues to be cool, but it won't last long I'm sure. I have lost a lot of weight. I am now down to 123. Just three more pounds and I will be at my normal weight of 120.

Thursday, June 22, 1944

The weather was just right today so I wore my new tangerine suit. Robert and I saw "The White Cliffs of Dover," a beautiful movie.

The news reel was riveting as well. General Mark Clark was filmed coming into Rome. Those beaming, shouting Italians were crowding all around the general's jeep. It was really a sight to thrill any American.

Saturday, June 24, 1944

I'm fairly "chomping at the bit" in anticipation of my vacation. I really felt slap-happy all day. I heard from Mother. She got my golf sticks out and polished them up for me. What a dear she is.

I do so hope that one day I too will be able to be a loving mother to a daughter. A son would be nice. I do enjoy spending time with Carl. But you know the old saying, "A son's a son till he takes a wife, a daughter's a daughter all your life."

Robert is such a dear. He told me I only had to work three hours tomorrow in order for me to get ready for my trip. He is so in love with me. No other man will quite take his place. And that is as it should be. He is my first true love. I would wish that he would be my only love.

The Honorable Thomas E. Dewey, Governor of the State of New York, was nominated on the first ballot as Republican nominee for President. Mr. Dewey is speaking now very fervently about the war. Willkie is no doubt listening and remembering another night four years ago.

I went to dinner and the movies with the Muntons. I told Carl not to get in any fights over the election. He is for Roosevelt who undoubtedly will run for a fourth term.

Sunday, July 25, 1944

My leave taking was exciting as usual. Robert took me out to dinner to the Watergate Inn. We have been going there for so long that I feel as though I belong to a private club when we walk through the door. Charles, the maitre'd, always says, "Good evening Miss Peters, and how are you tonight, Colonel? Shall I seat you at your usual table, or would you like to have a cocktail at the bar?" I simply love that.

When he took me to the train I cried when we said goodbye. I just couldn't help it. I love him so much.

Monday, July 26, 1944

Home again, home again. I had the best night sleep in my old bed. Mother and I gabbed all morning discussing creams, lotions, powders and clothes. What fun! It is quite warm here, but there is a breeze which is lacking in Washington. I remember when I was little I would call it "flying weather." I would stretch my arms out wide and shut my eyes and pretend that the breeze rushing across my face was lifting me up propelling me through the night sky.

Jake called me long distance. He seems to be doing well. He misses me and longs to see me. He said that there isn't a girl he's seen that can hold a candle to me. What a boy.

Tuesday, July 27, 1944

I woke up with the "curse" two days early for the third time. Only slight cramps. I stayed in bed until late afternoon. What luxury!

We ate out on the screened in porch every day for lunch and dinner. I love the sounds that our neighborhood makes in the summer. I could hear mother's voices calling their children in for dinner, and the children complaining, "Just five more minutes? Please?" There are the crickets and the cicadas singing to each other. Mr. Benson on the next block will play his guitar after dinner and it carries throughout the neighborhood.

It's all so lovely and serene and secure to me at home. I think I'll take a nice long tub before I go to sleep. You always sleep better after having a long bath. I won't wash my hair though. I don't want to sleep with wet hair.

Wednesday, July 28, 1944

I took it easy this morning, but went over to see my old friend Janice. She is working at The Sample Dress Shop four or five evenings a week, a nice way to pick up some extra money. She hinted that her boyfriend, Mike Lacotta, is going to propose soon. He's not in the war since he hurt himself when he was just a kid. He broke his leg riding on the back of the ice truck and it wasn't set right. He walks with a limp, but you don't really notice it that much. Janice can't wait to be a wife and mother, she told me. Mike's a nice boy.

I was able to get a little golf in today with Margaret Ahern. She's the girl I used to work with at the real estate office before I left for Washington. It was so nice to see her. Her game is much better than mine. To be fair, she's had more chances to play.

I called on Mrs. Brown this evening. As usual the conversation drifted to politics. She is absolutely for Dewey and thinks Roosevelt is out for a fifth and sixth term. I call Mrs. Brown an arch-Republican.

Lt. General Leslie J. McNair, formerly Commanding General of Army Ground Forces has been killed in action in Normandy. This is a great loss. He is the highest ranking Army Officer ever to have been killed in action in our casualty's history. Col. Munton always said he was the greatest general officer next to Marshall.

Jake called me tonight. He sounds very happy. I wrote to him before I went to bed. It's funny the things I can write to Jake about that I would never discuss with Col. Munton. I wrote to Jake about how I love the smell of sea grass, and how I've made a braid of it to let dry. And how in the depths of winter I will take that braid out and breathe in the sweet cinnamon smell of summer.

One night, around Christmas, we sat up late at Mrs. Nelson's and discussed the color of snow, how sometimes it can almost appear to be a shimmering soft blue. Then, in January, it can be an icy white. We just sat in front of the fire and talked without analyzing every thought. It was effortless and beautifully comfortable.

Col. Munton could never take the time to consider such frivolous thoughts.

Thursday, July 29, 1944

he allies have taken Cherbourg. A lot of people think the war will be over in Europe by September. I don't think so. We are not doing so well on the Island of Saipan in the Mariana Islands in the Pacific.

Margaret asked me to meet her for cocktails at The Lafayette Bar this evening. It's very nice there. She was asking me if there are many interesting and eligible men in Washington. I had to admit there are. The daiquiris at The Lafayette are simply wonderful. I wondered out loud what they do differently. The bartender was an older gentleman and decided he wasn't going to take his recipe to the grave. He confided in us that the biggest secret is plenty of ice to shake, and always pour it into a chilled glass.

Deborah's Daiquiris Recipe
- 1 1/2 ounces light rum
- 1 ounce fresh lime juice
- 1 teaspoon simple syrup or superfine sugar

Friday, July 30, 1944

Mother is devastated over my leaving. This vacation simply whizzed by. I didn't really get a chance to spend much time with Dad. He was at work all week of course. Dad took me to the train station as usual because it's too difficult for Mother to say goodbye there.

It occurred to me as I looked over at Dad behind the wheel, what a good man he is. He's thoughtful, kind and honest and he has such integrity. He's the most decent man I know. How lucky Mother is. Robert was on the platform to meet me. He has lost twelve pounds. We breakfasted at the Hot Shoppe. Everyone was glad to see me at the office.

Wednesday, August 2, 1944

Col. Munton put in for a request for me to go to Ocean Grove, New Jersey with Mrs. Munton and the children. I'm to tag along to keep Lily occupied. Permission was granted as long as it's okay with Maureen. I just pray that I can go. Mother and Dad would tell me stories about when they would visit there when they were young. It sounds like heaven.

Thursday, August 3, 1944

Everything is set for me to go to Ocean Grove. I'm so thrilled.

I worked three hours tonight and came home to find a present from Jake, six lovely lace hankies of Irish Linen. He called me up to see how I liked them. He won't get a furlough, as all leaves are cancelled until after December. Can you imagine!

I think this will be the last cool night for a while. Another hot spell is in the offering.

Friday, August 4, 1944

I went down to the Pentagon ticket office to pick up my return ticket to D.C. from Ocean Grove. Miss Vicellio, the girl who usually waits on me, is on her own vacation. I always like to watch her work. She is the typical American beauty. Very neat and shining all the time.

A couple of the girls from the office and I went to see a revival movie of the early 30's. Paul Muni in "Scarface" a story of our gangster era. Very terrific.

I have to make certain not to forget to take my new bathing suit. I'd hate to be at the beach and not be able to swim.

Sunday, August 6, 1944

Robert caddied nine holes for me at the Army War College. I had several good shots. He was very impressed. It's such a lovely place to play golf. You can watch the sail boats on the river. We went for a cocktail afterwards.

Monday, August 7, 1944

General McNair's only son Col. Douglas McNair has been killed on Guam. A whole family wiped out in two weeks. How Mrs.

McNair can go on living is more than I can fathom. She hasn't seen a doctor and made a statement to the press: "Pride in my men sustains me."

The war in Europe is going well. We are sweeping on towards Paris.

I packed my suitcase tonight. I am staying at the Munton's for a week prior to leaving for the shore.

Tuesday, August 8, 1944

I had dinner at the Greystone. I ironed a lot of undies tonight. It is so wonderful to iron on a nice ironing board. And, of course they have a laundry room. I wish Mother did.

Truly one never appreciates the comforts of home until one lives in a boarding house.

I am sleeping in Carl's room. It is full of model airplanes. Carl and Mrs. Munton left for the shore this morning.

Wednesday, August 9, 1944

Lily, Col. Munton, and I went to the movies and it was awful. I'm sick of these class B pictures. I am now down to a svelte 120 pounds. It seems good to have a nice slim figure again. Thank goodness Robert pointed me in the right direction towards watching my figure. I'm keeping my tan up by sun bathing in the Pentagon Court.

Thursday, August 10, 1944

Anne McDonald, Col. Howard's lady Marine secretary, took me to dinner at the Marine mess at Henderson Hall. Such food and all you want steak, scalloped potatoes, corn, string beans, bread and butter, celery pickles, deviled eggs, cherry cobbler, ice cream and punch. You eat off tin trays with divisions for the food. After eating you scrape the food off into a barrel. I went through the barracks which are spotless.

Friday, August 11, 1944

It is getting hot again. What a blessing to be here at the Munton's. Lily graduated today and Col. Munton took her to the movies tonight. I felt they should have a special evening to themselves. I decided to stay home and read.

Saturday, August 12, 1944

I picked up some mail from home. I got a letter from Mother and Dad. I'm reading "Mr. Skeffington." It is excellent. I hope the picture is at Ocean Grove while we're there. It is so much fun being here. These days are really perfect.

The heat today was awful. I have been sleeping in just a pair of panties. I washed and ironed and was so uncomfortable. Col. Munton was out house hunting today. He promised Mrs. Munton that she could have the house of her dreams.

I read out in the yard and got more tan.

Monday, August 14, 1944

I helped Lily pack her suitcase for the trip. She also told me what I should take. It seems to me I am taking a lot of clothes, but Lily says to have two changes a day. She's very used to going on trips and packing her bags and knowing what to take, and what not to take with you. She's gone on many trips with her mother.

We had to rush to the station but "Cheerful Cherub" Col. Munton got us there with two minutes to spare.

Lily and I had some amusing experiences on the trip. I was taken for her 18 or 19 year old sister. It was the dirtiest train ride from Trenton to Asbury Park. Lily had an episode with a drunk in Trenton. I had to intercede.

After we arrived and unpacked, Lily took me on the Boardwalk at night. It's quite exciting. We rode in a paddle boat and then we went in a fun house and haunted railway. I know we're going to have a grand time here; there's so much to do. I can see why Col.

Munton wanted me to come and help Mrs. Munton. I think the children would be too much for her on her own. I'm happy to do it.

I have to get some cotton candy. I can't remember the last time I had any. And I want to ride as many rides as I can. Who knows when I'll get the chance to be young again?

A young soldier sat next to me on a bench tonight when I took a short walk by myself. He said he was on leave and said that it felt good to be in a place that was all about fun and having a good time. He looked as though he had been through something, but then he asked me if he could kiss me. Can you imagine that? He played the old card, "These are unusual times. With war looming over us we have to live for the moment." What a play! No one falls for that anymore.

The kids were waiting up for me and we played cards and listened to the radio before we went to bed.

Wednesday, August 16, 1944

I had my first Ocean dip. Those white waves breaking on you are beyond description. I went swimming in the morning and the afternoon. There were loads of people on the beach.

I saw Bette Davis and Claude Rains in "Mr. Skeffington," which was excellent. Claude Rains is my favorite actor ever since I saw him in the "Invisible Man" years ago. This, of course, is for his acting ability alone. I believe he is a short man, and I truly adore tall leading men.

We have "pal-ed up" with a charming Scots woman and her twelve year old son, Mrs. McCabe and Tommy. They are real people.

Thursday, August 17, 1944

Another hot day. It must be unbearable in D.C. Mrs. McCabe and I swam beyond the ropes this morning at low tide while Lily kept an eye on Tommy. It is frowned upon to do so, but I do tend to push the boundaries. It was such fun. The waves take so much out of you; it is a relief to swim once in a while.

Mrs. Munton, Carl, Lily, Mrs. McCabe, Tommy and I went on the Boardwalk tonight. I played miniature golf. Tommy, Lily and I went for all the thrill rides, the "whip" and the "airplanes" being the most exciting. All of the kids said how brave I was and that I'm up for anything. Both of the mothers sat on the bench and watched us kids have fun. I didn't eat the cotton candy though. I have to keep watching my figure.

Friday, August 18, 1944

It rained this morning so I wrote a letter to Mother and Dad. The weather was cool, but sunny in the afternoon so Mrs. McCabe and I went swimming. It's more fun watching the other people on the beach. There is one little blonde boy I like to watch particularly. I call him "The Mischief."

I told his mother what a cute little boy I thought she had. How very lucky she is. I think I'd like to have a little girl first and then two boys. Mother and I are so close. I think every mother should have a daughter. The two sons would be an extra bonus. Although I don't believe I could ever watch them go off to war. Hopefully the next generation won't have to.

Tommy McCabe is the nicest 12 year old boy I've ever met. Mrs. McCabe says I am a great favorite of his. We all played 36 holes of miniature golf tonight by the light of the yellow bulbs strung around the little course. You could hear the waves crashing onto the shore. That's a wonderful soothing sound to go to sleep by.

Saturday, August 19, 1944

I went swimming morning and afternoon. Had a lot of fun with Tommy in the water. I took a splinter out of his foot, and he was very brave.

Mrs. McCabe, Tommy, Lily and I saw "Bathing Beauty" tonight. Nearly died laughing at Red Skelton's imitation of a girl getting up in the morning. We're all having such a good time. I don't want it to ever end.

I have to make sure to send Mother and Dad some postcards. I should send some to Mrs. Nelson as well.

Sunday, August 20, 1944

Going to church this morning was horrible. The preacher was ranting and making everyone feel as though they had sinned constantly and that our souls were lost. Really! What does he know about sinning? We parted with the McCabe's after a last turn around the Boardwalk. I am invited to visit them in Rochelle Park, New Jersey. What lovely new friends they are. Poor Tommy looked crestfallen when I gave him a kiss on the cheek goodbye.

I had a hair raising trip back to D.C. I got off at Princeton by mistake and if it wasn't for a quick thinking sailor I never would have gotten back on the train in time.

I talked to a very interesting lady inthe diner car. She lived in occupied China for a long time and got back to this country in October of 1941.

Everyone at work, especially Col. Munton, thinks I have

a marvelous tan. It really is super, but it won't be long before it wears off.

Tuesday, August 22, 1944

I am staying at the Munton's. It will be so hard to go back to the boarding house. I really want to get an apartment of my own. Even Mother and Dad feel it would be a good idea, but can I afford it?

I'm so tired I haven't yet recovered from the trip back.

Paris was liberated today, captured by French soldiers and patriots. Paris has been occupied by German forces since June of 1940.

I have decided that I am going to go to Paris someday. Maybe I will even live there. I know it must be beautiful. I want to be able to use my French. I can see myself buying flowers in a small shop and heading off to my lovely apartment. I will be eating delicious cheese, warm bread and heady wine across the table of a disarming, and very charming man, but who will that man be? I worked so hard to learn how to speak French. Yes, that is a goal.

Friday, August 25, 1944

There is no doubt that I shall be moving from Mrs. Nelsons. There are so many places advertised in the paper that it is bewildering. I don't know what I want really. That's the whole trouble. I don't want to jump from frying pan into the fire. If I make a change I want to be sure it's a good one. It certainly would be nice for Robert and me. We saw a movie tonight, "Two Girls and a Sailor," which was very good. It's funny; I thought to myself, I'm rather like that premise, only I'm two soldiers and one girl.

I got a call from Jake tonight. His assignment is up for change or renewal around September 6. He doesn't really know what will happen next. There is such uncertainty everywhere. People can't really make plans the way they used to before the war. No one knows what tomorrow will bring.

These days with Robert are lovely. I love him so terribly much. Without him I feel alone and lost. I get so depressed sometimes wondering what is going to happen to me. It is a very foolish and weak minded thing to do.

Friday, September 1, 1944

I went to Mrs. Miller's for dinner tonight; lamb chops, baked potatoes, squash, lettuce, onion and tomato salad and peaches and cake for dessert. Oh how I love the peaches this time of year, so sweet. We talked over everything. The allies are almost into Germany. It is the swiftest advance in military history. Mrs. Miller and I talked until 10:00 p.m.

I wrote to Mother how sweet her friend has been to me. She makes sure that I don't go without dinner and that I'm never lonely. Of course I certainly have that covered.

Saturday, September 2, 1944

Mrs. Nelson has offered me two rooms upstairs and a bathroom. I can use one of the rooms as a sitting room for entertaining. It's only $30.00. I think I'm going to take it. Moving is so much work. Somehow my radio is on the blink. What a time not to have a radio, especially with our troops going in to Germany.

I received a grand letter from Mrs. McCabe. She was very pleased with the pictures of our vacation. Her husband wants her to take Tommy to Washington for a weekend in October. She asked my opinion. She also wanted to know if I could get any time off while they are here. I shall write and tell her to plan on coming. I should like nothing better than showing them around my town.

I worked on my Washington scrap book tonight; so many memories, such a short time, such a long time.

Wednesday, September 6, 1944

Today was Henry (our colored messenger's) last day at the office. He is going to college in Richmond. As he is a preacher, we gave him a lovely leather bound Bible as a parting gift. Col. Munton gave a grand farewell speech, as only he can, and Henry was all smiles.

I've never in my life known of people coming and going so much. I'll make a friend and they'll move, or be sent away.

When we had a few moments to steal for ourselves I told Robert that his love was the crowning glory of my life. I hope it always will be.

Thursday, September 7, 1944

I went shopping tonight. I'm getting grand ideas for Christmas presents. I bought Mother "Sleeping" bath powder and soap (cologne wasn't in), and got Dad a set of Courtley's aftershave lotion and powder.

I got a letter from my cousin Carol, and she is coming here October 2nd, or 3rd, after spending a couple of days with her steady, Joe, in New York. It looks like everything happens at once. October is going to be my month alright for entertaining. How lucky I am that I made the move upstairs.

Friday, September 8, 1944

Lovely cool weather. I am wearing a coat, but as yet haven't gotten my suits out of the moth proof bag yet.

I worked two extra hours tonight. I feel so lost without a radio, not getting the war news as it comes in.

I wrote to Mrs. McCabe urging her and Tommy to come. Col. Munton says I won't have to work that Sunday and have Saturday afternoon off.

There is so much here for them to see. I'll have to make a list. I'll write to Mrs. McCabe and ask her what they want to visit most.

Sunday, September 10, 1944

It was such a lovely day, Col. Munton and I walked around the Pentagon before going to work. Afterward we he had a dinner engagement so I stayed at the Pentagon for dinner and wrote to Jake.

It is so beautiful here in September. If I do ever get married that is the month I would choose. It's not conventional and neither am I.

Monday, September, 11, 1944

The past walked into the office today in the person of Col. Baker who looks very fit after a year in the field. He was given a rousing welcome and blushed all over the place.

Col. Munton was very worried tonight over the apparent move by the anti-aircraft artillery to dominate Headquarters Army

Ground Forces. This is most dangerous and would affect the best interests of our country in the final analysis.

Col. Munton expects to go to the field about the first of the year, or in the spring. I wrote Carol tonight and said I was fortifying myself so as to accept the blow with "courage and grace."

I received a letter from Mother including three excellent snapshots of Carol, Laura and I, taken outside of their home when I was home in July.

Laura sent me a book of three short novels by James M. Cain, all of which are good.

Wednesday, September 13, 1944

It has been raining off and on for two days now. It is a change and I do love the rain. I have since I was a child.

War News:

We, the allies, have gone into Germany at three different points. The whole front in miles is no wider than the distance from here to New York City. Everyone is really optimistic about the war and feels that it will end this month. I do not share that view. It may be quite some time yet.

Robert and I stopped in at the Trans-Lux Newsreel Theatre and saw the liberation of Paris pictures. The street fighting is terrific. Also saw pictures of the Nazi death chambers under the streets of Paris.

Friday, September 15, 1944

Well the inevitable is here at last. I just found out today. Col. Baker is Col. Muntons replacement. He certainly can't be as good as Col. Munton in the job. He's had little staff experience and doesn't know anything else but coast artillery. From my point of view I could do worse. At least I know Col. Baker and his ways.

So much is happening and my head is whirling, but I have to remain steadfast for Robert. He needs me now.

I received a radio and an iron from Mother.

Saturday, September 16, 1944

Col. Munton won't know where he is to go until October 1st. He also doesn't know his assignment yet. I told mother last night that I thought he should be General commanding an artillery division . I wrote them how I feel about this turn of events. Not everything I feel, of course.

Sunday, September 17, 1944

I worked a couple of hours. I'm getting things set up for Col. Baker to move in. Believe me, I'm going to have to fight to keep back the tears the first week or two Col. Munton is gone. Oh my heart.

Mrs. McCabe and Tommy plan on coming to D.C. the 7th of October. Mother says Carol is coming here, but the date is indefinite. I don't know what to do. I feel so lost and blue.

The allies have landed an airborne army in Holland.

Wednesday, September 20, 1944

I called Mother today and asked if Carol could tell me when she is coming. I've got to let the McCabe's know. I'm all in a dither of course with Col. Munton about to take off and all the guests landing here practically at once. It is not a situation to make for peace of mind.

I worked two hours tonight. The last days with Col. Munton I am appreciating to the utmost.

Friday, September 22, 1944

They are selling special boxes for overseas. Christmas presents in the dime stores now filled with little treasures. This is certainly convenient for people. Everything in the U.S. is streamlined, even in war.

I worked a couple of hours. Well, it won't be very long before Robert will be gone. We have had beautiful two years together, golden days they were. In any dark days that may lie ahead I have a great deal to look back on and be thankful for.

Saturday, September 23, 1944

I got all the gifts wrapped and they fit perfectly in the regulation size box. I had the most harried letter from Jake yesterday. He is fed up with the army. It was one gripe from beginning to end and I am getting sick of his tune.

Col. Munton would never think to complain.

Sunday, October 1, 1944

I simply haven't been able to write a word in my diary for days. My heart is aching so. I guess I'm glad that I have guests coming in to town to keep my mind off of my sadness. Carol is coming on the 4th, and the McCabe's are coming in on the 14th. My dear Robert secured a room for the McCabe's. What will I do without him?

It's a poem of a day; sapphire blue sky, Indian summer, soft breeze. These last days with Robert are precious. I have no doubt that I will survive his leaving, but ah, the pain of the severing.

Tuesday, October 3, 1944

We worked late last night and tonight. Love is a wonderful thing. Although I get depressed about Robert going away, I know it is for the best. He could not stay forever. It is the changes in life which bring adventure. I am trying so hard to cultivate an acceptance of change. I know I can spare myself much unhappiness if I learn this now while I am young.

Robert is so wise. He tells me to stay strong and be a good soldier.

Wednesday, October 4, 1944

I was expecting a telegram from Carol all day, but she landed here at 3:30 p.m. She taxied right to the house. I was late getting home, so much work going on. Col. Munton brought her to the boarding house. She looks lovely and very happy. We had dinner at the Mayflower Hotel and talked most of the night in our room.

I broke down and had some milk and cookies when I got home. Mrs. Nelson had made them earlier in the day and the house smelled too delicious for words. I ate more than I should have I'm sure. I simply couldn't resist. I'm so tired.

Thursday, October 5, 1944

Carol and I had dinner at the Iron Gate tonight and then went to see "Double Indemnity." Very well acted, not sure if I like Barbara Stanwyck with blonde hair though. Fred MacMurray played a great insurance salesman. Speaking of insurance, Harry Rogers is here this week and I am taking out a $5,000 policy. Dad suggested it.

Friday, October 6, 1944

Col. Munton took Carol and me to dinner at Pierre's. Carol told of all her experiences at the State Hospital, gruesome to say the least. I would never have guessed that she would have become a nurse when she was growing up. She could never stand the sight of blood. I guess she got over it.

We all had a long talk about the pitfalls of marriage. Carol and I had more fun in my room tonight. Got into a giggling spell. I tried on one of her up-lift brassieres and she tried on one of mine that doesn't do anything. Carol seems to be really in love with Joe.

Saturday, October 7, 1944

I brought Carol up to the office and introduced her around. She was particularly impressed by Col. Gray our British officer.

We paid $3.00 per person to see Ethel Barrymore in "Embezzled Heaven." Her acting was wonderful, but we didn't like the play.

Sunday, October 8, 1944

I can hardly believe it, Wendell Willkie, my favorite American, died of a heart attack this morning.

Carol and I enjoyed a lovely day in Alexandria. We had dinner at "The Old Club." We walked around the city and she listened to my story. She said she could feel my heart breaking and wished that there was something she could say.

Monday, October 9, 1944

Col. Munton and I put Carol on the train at 8:00 a.m. There was this movie, "Love Affair," with Irene Dunne and Charles Boyer, and in the movie one of the characters says, "I hate boat whistles," when she hears the far of sound signaling the end of a lovely visit. I feel the same way about train whistles. I didn't want to see Carol leave. I don't know when, or if, she'll be back again.

I thought all day long about Willkie. He died at the peak of his career. The world has lost a great man, but what he stood for is living still. All the eulogies by prominent people from President Roosevelt on down were wonderful.

I wonder if in my life there will ever be a man on the political scene who stirs me as Wendell Willkie did?

Tuesday, October 11, 1944

I received a letter from Mrs. McCabe. She and Tommy are not coming to Washington owing to the expense of only two days. Although I am disappointed I can see her point.

I had a letter from Mother. She is trying to persuade me to vote for Dewey.

I saw the Munton's new house tonight. It is darling. The back yard is especially nice with a swinging gate and a rock garden. I can see how Mrs. Munton brings everything together so easily. She knows how to make a house a home.

I helped them by cleaning the bookcase and linen closet shelves. All this work made me so hungry I could eat a horse. I made myself a big sandwich when I got home.

Sunday, October 15, 1944

It's a jewel of a day. I do so love October. The Muntons have several oak trees in their back yard and I offered to rake their leaves. The smell is so pungent and fresh. There are also pine trees, and the mix of pine needles with the oaky leaves is lovely. Carl asked if we could make a bon-fire at the end of the day. Col. Munton was against it, but I convinced him. I loved the crackle of the fire and the popping sound of moisture in the sticks.

Before I left, Mrs. Munton asked if I could help put the books on the shelf. I noticed that she had a copy of "Rebecca" by Daphne Du Maurier and I asked if I could borrow it. Of course I had seen the movie, but I had never gotten around to reading the book. Books are always so much better. She said, yes, and that I should keep it as a thank you for helping them put the house together. I'm going to read it when I get back to the house. It's a perfect book to read this time of year, and my clothes smell like the woods, earth and autumn.

I noticed before I walked out the door how their furniture shows off much better in the new house.

Exactly four years ago today, Mother and Dad and I heard Willkie at The Memorial Auditorium. Time is going by so quickly. Four years ago I doubt I would have dreamt that I would be living in Washington and working at the Pentagon. It would have been too fantastic of a dream.

Tuesday, October 17, 1944

Col. Munton and I walked over to the Hot Shoppe for dinner. It was a gorgeous evening. The lagoon scene in front of the Pentagon is worth a camera shot.

I got a letter from Jake. He has "ants in his pants" again and wants to go back to India. Never satisfied. That's why he remains a corporal in my opinion.

Our Navy is doing well in the Pacific. The Japs fleet is still afraid to fight.

Friday, October 21, 1944

All of the Sundays in October have been beautiful, grand autumn days. I have always loved this time of year, but now it means the end of something beautiful. Spring was two years ago for me, now it is the autumn of our relationship.

I worked three hours today with Robert. I want to keep my mind on my work. It's such important work. I have to realize that my country needs me to remain focused. I wonder what I'll be doing with my Sunday's when he's goes away.

Sunday, October 23, 1944

I had dinner with a new girl in the office, Louise. She invited me to see her room and suggested that I move into her boarding house. It is lovely, but the rooms would not accommodate my possessions. The single rooms are too small and the double and triple rooms are too crowded. Boarding is inconvenient from my stand point. I'll be going to the Munton's twice a week. Robert feels his family will need me while he is away. I feel so honored the way he relies on me so. I'm so young, yet he sees me as a woman of sustenance.

Robert said that Mrs. Munton and the children want me to continue to be a part of their lives while he is away as well. Helping him in this way will give me the opportunity to continue to be a part of his life.

161

There is a path for me that Robert is setting. It may not be the path I would have decided upon, but he is so much wiser than I.

I have to ask Mother to send me some strawberry jam, and I just know she'll put some of her pumpkin bread in with it if I ask. I do miss Mother's cooking so, especially at this time of year. Its such comfort food, and I do need comforting right now.

Tuesday, October 31, 1944

October Night

The autumn leaves they tumble down
The sultry air it fills the night,
A wistful moon it made a crown
Of beauty everywhere in sight
We walked among the rustling leaves
They whispered of a slumbering love
The moon and stars they seem to call
To us and say Take back your long lost love
When old October comes again
To clothe the world in loveliness
Then we'll be walking down the lane
In one brief hour of breathlessness
The memory of that perfumed night
Is ours to share forever more
And it will burn with poignant light
Although our paths may cross no more
                    Deborah Peters

October 1944

Halloween was always such a fun night for me when I was young. I didn't even realize that today was Halloween until I put my head on my pillow. Mother used to make the best costumes for me.

And Oh! The candy apples were the best. What an innocent time that was for all of us.

Jake called long distance. He has been trying to get an honorable discharge from the army. He lost his temper with a psychiatrist. His CO is going to recommend his transfer to Washington. I can see where I'm going to have a lot to contend with.

Cousin Laura called me tonight. The sister of one of her boyfriends, I've met her once or twice, is meeting her boyfriend in Washington this weekend. She can't seem to get a hotel reservation and wants to know if it's possible for her to stay with me Saturday night. I said of course it would be alright.

Saturday, November 4, 1944

Laura's friend, Debbie, came in tonight. Her train was two hours late and her boyfriend was frantic. They went to dinner at the Hot Shoppe. I felt that would be in their budget. She didn't come in until after 1:00 a.m. I totally understand. Spending time with the man you love is something I will always be able to have empathy for.

She'll be leaving tomorrow afternoon. A long trip for such a short stay, but when your boyfriend is a soldier and his leave is measured in hours rather than days, you do what you have to do. No one knows this more than I.

Laura sent me a note of thanks for helping her friend; she also included a box of my favorite chocolate filled with cream from Parkside Candy. I'm going to have to make sure to share them with everyone. I don't want to put anymore pounds on. It was so thoughtful of Laura.

Tuesday, November 7, 1944

Mrs. Miller entertained tonight to hear the election returns. It was a riot. It was a mixed crowd, Dewey and Roosevelt supporters were there in equal measure. We kept score on election charts. At 10:00 it was obvious Roosevelt would win. I am very pleased, naturally, that my first vote in a Presidential election was on the winning side. Mrs. Miller invited me to spend the night. It was so sweet of her to ask me. We stayed up rather late celebrating.

One thing is for certain. This is no time to change presidents.

Wednesday, November 8, 1944

All of the votes aren't in yet, but the President got a huge electoral vote, over 400. He took New York, Pennsylvania, Illinois and California, just as I thought he would. The Democrats gained 22 seats in the House. I'm glad that F.D.R. has a congress with him that will help a lot.

Thursday, November 9, 1944

I went to bed early only to be awakened by a phone call from Col. Munton. I forgot to lock the safe and Major Kelly evidently didn't check it. A guard found it opened and joint security control was all agog. Col. Munton was pretty mad.

I do so hope he doesn't hold on to his anger, which he has every right to do. This is no ordinary job that I have.

Friday, November 10, 1944

The Nazis are still offering stiff resistance in Italy, France and Germany. It will be spring at the latest probably before they will give up. I found out that Col. Munton won't be leaving for a month.

I stayed up late tonight to write to Mother and Dad. I washed out a few things. I'm truly trying to keep my spirits up. Robert is alive when so many soldiers have fallen. He is still on this earth and this I need to be grateful for.

I haven't heard from Jake lately. I wonder what's wrong. He's no doubt very mad at me for not writing.

Friday, November 17, 1944

Today is Robert's and my second anniversary. He gave me the Robin Red nail polish and lipstick I asked for, and he has another present he's going to give me for "good conduct." The shape of the box looks like perfume.

We dined at The Watergate Inn, Charles knew that it was our anniversary, as there were complimentary cocktails waiting for us at "our" table. I opened the other present before dinner. It was a token set of lipstick with perfume and enclosed a perfume refill. I am thrilled with it.

Gladys, the little maid girl in the office, recommended Sulphur ointment as a cure for "hickies." I got some and it really works.

Tuesday, November 21, 1944

It is quite cold out today. The fighting is hard all over the world. It doesn't look too good. The way the newspapers play up the optimistic view slays me.

Col. Munton heard today he might be Executive of the 32nd Corps Artillery at Fort Bragg, N.C. I was very proud of myself. I did not wince when he told me the new.

I didn't receive any mail today. There is an acute shortage of popular brand cigarettes. Even in the Pentagon you can't get any. Now that's bad.

I worked late tonight. Robert and I had a long talk in the car tonight. I am going to try my darndest not to make a tragedy out of his leaving. I must not fail him. I want to come through with flying colors.

Thursday, November 23, 1944

Thanksgiving Day, but we had to work just the same. The Pentagon served a grand Thanksgiving dinner. The dressing was like Mother's. I had turkey in the evening too.

Jake called me today to wish me a Happy Thanksgiving. I guess he is over his being angry with me. He is back at his old job at Patterson field.

How long has it been since he's had a good old fashioned Thanksgiving dinner, or for that matter, Christmas dinner. Jake deserves to sit down and have a real feast. He deserves so much.

Saturday, December 2, 1944

Mrs. Munton came over to the Pentagon for lunch. Col. Munton asked me to go with them to the dining room where you order instead of waiting in line. I didn't feel much like eating though, so I stayed at my desk.

I ate some of my Parkside Candy tonight and read. I was going to wash my hair but decided against it.

Monday, December 4, 1944

The war for the U.S. is now three years old. We have come a long way, but still have a long way to go. The big job will be landing on the China Coast and getting the Japs out of there when they are so firmly entrenched.

I saw two war department films, "Brief for Invasion" and "German's Moral." They were gruesome. I always feel so humble after seeing those films. All the things I said to Robert about wanting to help him win this war are true.

Robert and I worked late tonight. These days are so exciting and full to the brim of life. This Washington experience, I wouldn't trade for assured security for the rest of my life.

Wednesday, December 13, 1944

Today is Robert's birthday. I gave him two gifts that could not be wrapped. A poem and stolen moments for us to love.

My Darling it's oh so hard to keep suppressed
this feeling that must be expressed
How very much I care for you
although sometimes you make me blue
Someday perhaps they'll all come true

166

These dreams I have regarding you;
But if the fates keep us apart,
I know down deep within my heart
There will always be a place for you;
my darling if you only knew
Yours Forever, Lady Hamilton

The weather is very cold, but in spite of it Col. Munton and I walked over to the Hot Shoppe for dinner and back. This exercise is good for both of us.

I am so happy that Robert will be here at least until January 15th. He is most dubious about the likelihood of a good assignment. Most of the good spots for colonels in combat are all taken. It will be a crime if he doesn't get something worthy of his ability.

Monday, December 18, 1944

I have not answered Jake's last two letters. They were so snippy I don't think they deserve answering.

I went to the movies with the Muntons and saw "The Conspirators" with Paul Henreid and Hedy Lamarr. Very exciting.

The news from Europe is bad. The Germans are landing a terrific counter attack and have penetrated twenty miles into Belgium. Their first troops have been committed to the engagement. Our first army is hard pressed in the attack.

These days are going by so quickly. I wish there was a way for me to make time stand still. I must keep these thoughts to myself, for I have no one to share them with. I wish Carol were here, I do so need someone to talk to.

Friday, December 22, 1944

Robert took me to the station. It wasn't as crowded as I thought it would be. Tomorrow night will probably be the big jam. Robert handed me a small, purple velvet box. When I opened it there were beautiful earrings; blue stone set in gold, sprinkled with rhinestones around the side.

The crowd getting on the coaches on my train was terrible. They are standing inside and on the platforms between the cars. We were fifteen or twenty minutes waiting, we will no doubt be late in the morning coming in.

I'm so looking forward to being home. It's such a safe and comforting sanctuary. At Christmastime there is no other place I would rather be. It's like when you were little and you were afraid and you would get under the covers and pull them up over your head. Nothing could get to you when you were under those covers. They were an impenetrable fortress.

Sunday, December 24, 1944

We opened our presents this morning. I love the smells and sounds of breakfast on Christmas morning: the coffee percolating, toast in the oven, bacon frying, eggs bubbling. It took a good hour and a half to finish opening all of the gifts. We are all excited over how well we did.

I got a black dress, gloves, stationery, nylon umbrella, cologne, bath powder, slippers, perfumed soap, bath oil, blouse, rhinestone earrings, hand crocheted mittens, white satin lace step-ins, and more. The dinner was perfect, as always. Never has our Christmas tree meant more to me. It speaks of home and warmth and love and security. How can that be so much to ask for, or to hope for?

Mother, Dad and I attended midnight mass. There was an extra beauty filling the church this year. All of the candles were lit and the smell of pine was everywhere. I love this sense of community. Buffalo is my home. People stay here, they make lives for themselves, create families. Washington is so transient.

You could see and feel so much despair and yet so much hope. I saw faces of families who I knew had lost loved ones in this wretched war. My heart aches for their loss, and yet the hope is still there. You can feel it, as well as see it in their faces. This is why we go on.

Monday, December 25, Christmas Day, 1944

It snowed today; a beautiful winter wonderland is the result. I opened my bedroom window and took in a big fresh breath of Christmas morning air. Jake called this morning to wish me a Merry Christmas. He had a jolly tone to his voice.

Mother made her famous eggnog and we invited the Browns over for a rollicking rendition of Jingle Bells. The Twelve Days of Christmas was next, and Dad was a riot with his, "FIVE GOLDEN RINGS." That's always his part.

Thursday, December 28, 1944

Lily Munton and I went to dinner and a show. It is a long involved story. The Strunk's had invited the Muntons for dinner. Gary Strunk is Lily's heartthrob, and he and his brother and sister were due to go to a dance right after dinner. This was rather insulting since Lily is of age and Gary has taken her out before. However they did not invite her to join them. So to "show him" Lily went out with me (I was supposed to be a boy who had asked her out). It worked out fine. I was her beard.

Friday, December 29, 1944

It is snowing out and so pretty. The first army has driven the Germans back twelve miles in Belgium. The tide seems to be turning.

Robert is so good to me. His devotion has never been equaled in history I think. I love him dearly and soon he will be gone. At twenty-four I have known a great love. Perhaps I shall never know another. I know it will never be like this at any rate.

Saturday, December 30, 1944

Went to dinner with the Muntons and then to a show. The movie was "Laura" with Gene Tierney. It was highly recommended to me by Maureen. Well it was perfect. Suspense all the way through.

Gene Tierney is such a beauty, and the music was so romantic. Her portrait over the fireplace was absolutely perfection. I so want to have my portrait painted. Maybe when I get to Paris.

Sunday, December 31, 1944

I had a lovely day with Robert. I showed him all my Christmas presents tonight. He stayed for a while and shared a glass of champagne with me. And then he was off to his party at his new home. He had invited me this year, but I declined. This is New Year's Eve and quite the quietest I have ever spent.

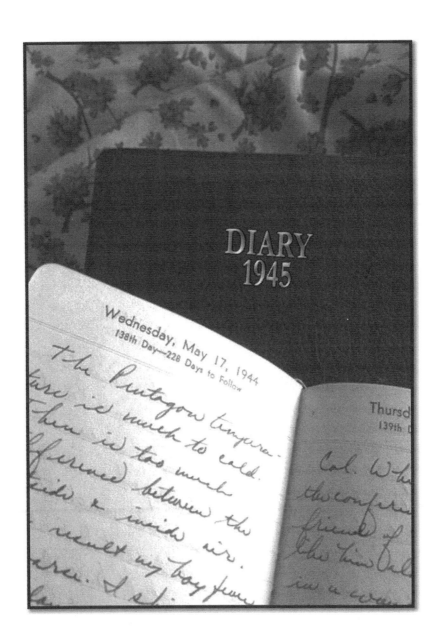

Monday, January 1, 1945

A work day as usual. I so wish that I was being sent with Robert to help him. A tiny bit of me was hoping for that. It was a Christmas wish that didn't come true.

Hitler made a speech last night in which he stated Germany would never surrender. We are surely in for a tough fight.

Robert and I had dinner tonight in my little sitting room. I told him all about being home for Christmas, how the table was set, how the tree glistened with tinsel and how all of the packages were placed neatly under the tree. We talked about simple things, nothing that would break the spell.

Right before he left and after he kissed me he told me that he had received his release date, February 1.

Friday, January 5, 1945

The war in Europe is bad. The Germans really mean business and I wouldn't be at all surprised if the European war dragged on into 1946. It is so cold there. I feel for our troops. It is terrible. War itself is bad enough without the bitter cold.

Robert and I saw "Wilson." I can't help but think how much we are repeating those times.

I worry about our President. He is being criticized today almost exactly as President Wilson was in 1916-1918. How can any man continue under such stress? I firmly believe that the same reactionary wave will sweep over our people after this war. It is a sad commentary on human nature that we don't benefit by the mistakes of the past. I hope and pray that I am wrong. I pray every day that our country remains strong. We cannot falter. If I have learned anything from being here it that we must band together. Robert never wavers. He is my strength.

I am so very tired of these long cold days.

Monday, January 8, 1945

Jake is coming here on furlough the first or second of February. We can have a swell time if there is no fighting, but I am dubious knowing Jake as I do. He is such a demanding person who wants his own way all the time. And he'll no doubt want to monopolize every bit of my time.

I do hope Robert is still here then. He can help me a great deal. I know I shall be able to count on him for aid and advice any time in my life, dear Robert!

My laundry box arrived. Mother included pictures of Buffalo's latest storm.

Wednesday, January 10, 1945

The weather is very cold lately. The scarf Mrs. Miller knitted for me for Christmas is coming in handy.

Congress is considering a National Service now which amounts to "work or fight" as far as 4Fs are concerned. Nurses are to be drafted under this law too. I hope Carol gets a good assignment if it comes to pass. Admiral King and General Marshall have requested that this law be passed. Personally, I think it should have gone through long ago.

Monday, January 15, 1945

I worked tonight. I have a lot on my mind these days, mostly imagination. I keep wondering if I'll be able to stay here after

Robert goes. It will be terribly lonely at first. The hard things will be eating alone, getting new interests, in other words, and an entirely new routine of living. It's a comfort to know that I have a home to go to if I can't stand staying here. I do want to stay here though. Life in Buffalo would be very dull after this, even Mother said so.

At the end of the day Robert came over and brought a bottle of wine and some cheese and bread. He said he has found out more about his assignment today. He is going to the Central Pacific by air due in San Francisco February 20th. I can't tell anyone until he finds out exactly what his assignment will be.

Wednesday, January 31, 1945

I had a letter from Dad today. They are still buried under drifts and drifts of snow. I worry about him shoveling. I wish he would hire some boy on the street to help him out. Mother and Dad haven't been to a movie since early December. There are miles of freight cars outside Buffalo which can't get into the station and unload. Carol graduates from nursing school tomorrow. I have to get something off to her.

Col. Munton is to be Executive of a Corps Artillery which is a honey of an assignment.

Thursday, February 1, 1945

I saw a very sad but excellently acted film with the Muntons, "Till We Meet Again" with Ray Milland and a very beautiful girl Barbara Britton. It was about a French nun and an American flyer in Nazi occupied territory. Neither Mrs. Munton nor the kids mentioned anything about Col. Munton going away. It's just as well.

I wonder if Jake will be here tomorrow. His furlough begins today. I have been thinking about Jake a great deal lately. I'm not sure how Col. Muntons departure is going to affect Jake and me. This will most certainly be a very telling time in my life. I feel like I'm on the brink of a very big decision.

Sunday, February 4, 1945

While I was at work I had a call from Jake. He has been transferred back to ATC, his furlough rescinded. He's not sure when, and if, he'll be coming to Washington any time soon.

Col. Munton took his physical exam and passed all but blood pressure. His is too high. It is not organic with him but a natural state. For his sake, I hope he can persuade the medics. He's to come back tomorrow for another check. He is going to walk to work which he hopes will help reduce his blood pressure.

Thursday, February 8, 1945

Col. Munton has passed his physical, blood pressure A-Okay. He received his orders today. He reports to Hamilton Field California by February 25.

Jake called and said he was definitely coming down to Washington tonight from New Castle, Delaware. I hate to say it, but I'll believe it when I see it.

I went down to the station to meet him. Really, I don't see how I ever could have been attracted to him. He never looked as Irish as he did tonight. We had dinner at the station. He was peeved that I was working tomorrow so he went up to New York on the 9:00 train. I was so relieved.

Sunday, February 11, 1945

Robert came over and took me out to lunch. He gave me a parting gift, pre-war imported "Christmas Night" by Caron in a black bottle. The box is beautiful with a green tassel.

Monday, February 12, 1945

Col. Munton is supposed to be on a ten day leave, but you'd never guess it. He's in and out of the office all the time.

The war is going well both in Europe and Asia. I have a hunch the Germans are going to hold out as long as they can. The party in power has no other choice.

Roosevelt, Churchill and Stalin are meeting in the Black Sea. It is reported that they have already decided on Germany's fate.

Col. Munton leaves for San Francisco a week from Wednesday. I went down and picked up his ticket today.

I went over to the Munton's to drop off his tickets and they asked me for dinner. We had fun playing "Society Craps."

We talked over the routine after Col. Munton leaves. I am to drive the car, take Mrs. Munton to the commissary and Clarendon twice a month. It will be a set-up for mutual benefit. Lily started crying tonight and I have no doubt she will have hysterics the night before he leaves.

Wednesday, February 14, Valentine's Day, 1945

Tonight was the most memorable Valentine's Day of all my life. Robert and I had our farewell party at the Shoreham Blue Room. I wore my good black dress, my hat with the veil and feathers, my rhinestone jewelry, and my squirrel jacket. We had a lovely dinner; shrimp cocktail, braised Swiss steak, daiquiris and ice cream. We danced and gazed into each other's eyes, perhaps for the last time. It was heart-wrenching, but of course it was divine.

Oh my darling Robert. I now know love like this could never be. He has given me peace and serenity. I am thoughtful while I am living through these days.

When we got in the car he kissed me, much like that first time on that cold November night two and a half years ago. He reached in the back seat and pulled out a box, a blue satin box tied with purple ribbon. There was a letter inside the box and a picture of the two of us that someone had taken at the last Christmas party. We both looked so happy. He took my hand and told me not to read the letter until after he had left.

Monday, February 19, 1945

I have decided to move out of Mrs. Nelson's. It's time for me to make some changes.

Robert and I had a long talk tonight. I just can't put into words how I feel. There is so little time for talk. I feel so rushed. I love him so. Why can't we marry? Would we be happy if we did? He's so much older than I am. Will I ever love again? How will this all end? In a life of frustrations - why? why? why?

Tuesday, February 20, 1945

Our Marine forces have landed on Iwo Jima 75 miles from Japan.

Col. Munton and I had our last dinner together at the Hot Shoppe. It seemed just like any other night. He said goodbye to the blonde lady hostess, Mrs. Wells, and the waitresses.

I am so thankful for all the wisdom and guidance he has given me. I shall try with every fiber of my being to live up to and be worthy of the trust he has in me. Life will be so strange at first without him.

I am giving him a volume of Laurence Hope's complete love lyrics as a going away gift. I wrote in the front "No sweet lover and no second child efface the memory of the first who came." This is the poem I marked for him to read alone:

177

Farewell

Farewell, Aziz, it was not mine to fold you
Against my heart for any length of days.
I had no loveliness, alas, to hold you,
No siren voice, no charm that lovers praise.

Yet, in the midst of grief and desolation,
Solace I my despairing soul with this:
Once, for my life's eternal consolation,
You lent my lips your loveliness to kiss.

Ah, that one night! I think Love's very essence
Distilled itself from out my joy and pain,
Like tropical trees, whose fervid inflorescence
Glows, gleams, and dies, never to bloom again.

Often I marvel how I met the morning
With living eyes after that night with you,
Ah, how I cursed the wan, white light for dawning,
And mourned the paling stars, as each withdrew!

Yet I, even I, who am less than dust before you,
Less than the lowest lintel of your door,
Was given one breathless midnight, to adore you.
Fate, having granted this, can give no more!

Wednesday, February 21, 1945

Col. Munton had dinner with his family, made his farewells and came back to the office about 9:30. I had determined to be gay and cheerful, and I was. We went to the train. We kissed goodbye in the dim light of car 73. My eyes were moist, but I didn't cry. I last saw him standing beside the train with his bags next to him. He gave me a two fingered salute and boarded the train. I turned and ran down the platform.

Tonight I feel I won a great victory over myself by not crying. Driving the car home I had a feeling of peace.

Deborah wrote very little in her diaries after Col. Munton left. She moved into a new apartment with another girl Mrs. Miller had known and suggested to her. From then on her diaries were filled primarily with important news of the war.

Thursday, April 12, 1945

I had just started dinner tonight when the phone rang. It was Mrs. Miller telling me tragic, almost unbelievable news; President Roosevelt has died of a cerebral hemorrhage at Warm Springs, Ga. I couldn't move. I stood by the stove with a spoon in my hand and it was as though my heart stopped, for just a second.

At 1:30 p.m. he complained of a dreadful headache, fainted, never regained consciousness, and died at 3:35 p.m. The whole freedom loving world is stunned by the passing of this great man. He died at a time of triumph for our armies. Our troops have crossed the Elbe and are almost to Berlin.

Friday, April 13, 1945

President Truman took the oath of office last night at 7:09. He recited the oath with a calm, determined voice, but his face was ashen.

I feel that our country, and the world, was dealt a heavy blow in the death of President Roosevelt. His knowledge of international affairs was unsurpassed. We pray God to guide President Truman in the hard and mountainous tasks ahead.

He has already issued his first order - the San Francisco Security Conference will open as scheduled. The streets of Washington are eerily silent tonight. People speak in heavy whispers. The grief is palpable. How could this happen now? Even the radio is in mourning for our president. Nothing but soft beautiful music.

Saturday, April 14, 1945

The President's body arrived in Washington at 10:00 a.m. A military funeral procession went from Union Station to the White House. Services were at 4:00 p.m.

People watching the procession cried unabashedly. We had a memorial service in the Pentagon Court at 12:30. All government agencies were off this afternoon, but I stayed because civilians and our officers had to remain on duty in each office.

A message from Shirley Wethey, wife of Lt. Col. H.D.W. Wethey, Royal Canadian Corps of Signals, to Ruby MacArthur:

"It is hard to realize, even now, that President Roosevelt is dead. We couldn't keep the tears back, and I know that Canadians everywhere feel they've lost someone beloved. I suppose that in Washington the sense of gloom would be still greater.

I remember so well the day he visited Kingston in 1938. There were very few permanent force officers at Vimy Barracks to form a guard. Louis Gagnon was one of them and saluted so smartly when Roosevelt got off the train, that he knocked his cap awry.

While the President was at Queens University, Louis, with our handful of officers, was whisked to the American side of the Ivy Lee

180

Bridge, and when the prime minister and the president drew up, they were on hand to welcome them. As Louis saluted once more, Roosevelt leaned out of the car and said to Louis, "What! Are you here again - how did you get here?

Louis turned sunset pink, while the great man grinned at him. How we teased Louis afterward, but these little things just endeared him to everyone and revealed his eye for detail."

I so appreciate Ruby sharing the letter with me. This is a perk of knowing all the secretaries. She said she will keep it always.

I feel so sorry for President Truman having to follow in the footsteps of anyone so wonderful. His address to Congress this morning was very good I thought."

Tuesday, May 1, 1945

Hitler is dead! It is not clear whether he died of a cerebral hemorrhage, or was killed at his command post. At any rate, Himmler has not taken over. An Admiral Donitz has, and there is a split in the Nazi ranks.

Commentator Raymond Gram Swing says this may prolong the war. It is interesting to note that President Roosevelt and Hitler, who ascended power in the same year 1933, died within a month of each other.

I feel as though we are teetering on the brink of great change, but what change will it be? We are all holding our breath to see what happens next. In what direction will our country, will our world, head?

Tuesday, May 8, 1945 VE Day!

I got up in time to hear President Truman and the glorious news! Everyone in the house listened to the radio all morning long. We flung open the windows and could feel, and hear, the joy throughout Washington, and indeed the world. We listened to Churchill, Harry Hopkins, Mrs. Roosevelt, General Patton, General Patch, General Hodges, General Simpson and others express their feelings and their joy. Mrs. Roosevelt's words were so comforting.

Mrs. Nelson cooked all day. She said that she knew that people would be coming in and out of the house all day long and she wanted to make sure they had something to eat. I was sent to the liquor store to stock up. This is a celebration like no other. I can't seem to get through to Mother and Dad. Of course everyone is calling everyone.

New York's Times Square was full of people, blocking traffic and tons of ticker tape. I can't begin to describe the emotion I am feeling. What pride I am bursting with. Our dear, dear country.

However, our little church on the corner was bright with light tonight, and many cars were parked on their yard. You could hear the soft prayers from hundreds of people of all faiths pouring out of the church. We are all very thankful, grateful and thrilled, but we are also thinking of Japan.

Tuesday, August 14, 1945

The day of jubilation!! Peace at last! At 7:00 p.m. President Truman let the newsmen announce that Japan had accepted the surrender terms. Almost immediately horns started to blow. Then Mrs. Miller came over and drove us downtown. Never will I forget the joyous crowds. The throngs of people in front of the White House were tremendous. Service men were riding on top of street cars, garbage can tops were banged against White House pillars, flags waving, horns blaring, scrap paper drifting down from buildings, traffic stopped on 14th Street, service men kissing every girl in sight. A two day holiday has been declared for all government employees. This is what Robert and I have worked and prayed for.

Deborah's Collected Letters
in the Blue Satin Box with
the Purple Ribbon

February 14th Valentine's Day 1945

From Colonel Robert Munton

My Dearest Beloved,

We knew this day would come, and we have prepared for it. It is most important to me that you know in your heart that this is not the end. As Lord Nelson and Lady Hamilton endured difficult times apart, so must we.

Our love has attained a growth approaching maturity. It is true that the customs and mores of our times have added handicaps to our lives. It is equally true that neither you nor I are capable of judging the wisdom of our decisions. This is a verdict of the future and of the Master. All one can do is evaluate the facts as honestly as possible, make a decision and adhere thereto valiantly. Doubt will assail us. This is to be expected and is a healthy sign evidencing our sincerity and vitality. Fears will attack us. So long as these fears center about the happiness and welfare of others, they are normal. Once these fears and doubts center about us, it is time to scrutinize our love. A few loves are immortal. We believe ours is among those few.

I love you dearest,

LN

December 11, 1946

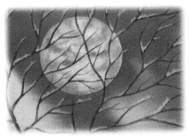

Japan
Baby, Baby!

Last night the moon was one of grace's "out of this world" realities. It was a creamy silver color and the atmosphere was of such texture that the skies seemed of pearly effluence - a form of back glow for the moon itself. This moon almost vied with the sun in brilliance and seemed to hang in suspense about halfway from the horizon. Some of the skies of Japan are unbeatable. The sunsets and moon rises are particularly impressive.

It is times like this that make me lonely. I want to feel you quietly and warmly within my arms and the snuggling caress of your cheek against mine as we both witness nature at her best.

My writing has gone into a tailspin. In fairness I cannot blame the arrival of the family for they have not rippled my routine. I have a very guilty feeling over mother, for I failed to write her Saturday as usual, and must get a letter off to her today. With the holiday season it is imperative that she not feel neglected or forgotten. I could do neither, but living persons need physical reminders of love or their minds drift to fearful fancies.

Good night My Lady of the Silver Dream - May your letter arrive today and release me from suspense - also release my thoughts for you. The office is stretching and sighing preliminary to the day's work a head. Soon my two Majors will breeze in and tackle their baskets with the aftermath of a cascade of papers for me to check and sign. I love this earth that bears you; I love the skies that smile upon you and all because

I love you,
Robert

December 12, 1946

My Beloved,

My darling I miss you terribly. But I am not selfish enough not to understand how important it is to spend this Christmas with your parents. My need is not so urgent that I cannot exist for this short period of time without you. You should endeavor to make them very happy this Christmas and orient their thoughts so that they are enthusiastic over your opportunity. Their actual fears are more for you than for themselves. They love you and sometimes they fear that tragedy or harm might befall their heart stone.

Also, take this opportunity to be the forelock and give each of your relatives and close friends that final fill up of pleasure so that their memories of you will be alive and loveable.

I can appreciate the nostalgia that touches you over leaving the Signal Corp. It was a battle ground for endeavor. After the smoke and dust settles one appreciates the interest and even the affection that encircled said battleground.

The peoples - both attractive and unattractive added their touch so that the Signal Corps gained a personality of its own. I, too, understand this fraternity of work. So long as life gives me reason my loyalty to the Signal Corps will be positive, as you will discover meeting Signal Corp personnel will reawaken that sense of "belonging" and provide you with many future hours of pleasant reminiscence and reunion.

My heart is in a dither. The day you set foot on Japan's soil will be a gala day. You will be engulfed by my arms and I am dreaming of those soft but firm lips answering the hunger that is with me. Keep a tight rein on expectation.

Lovingly yours,
LN

December 24, 1946

Christmas Eve
Mine Own Heart -

This is the Eve of Christmas. The eyes of my heart can see you, bubbling with joy and laughter, preparing for the dawn to come. Soon, very soon, it will be the dawn of Christmas. Wish - oh wish to the tiny fairies - that my lips could be the ones to awaken you from sleep with the dawn of Christ's Day. To see the glint of recognition slip into your eyes and the slow smile of love blazon within their depths would be the best of presents. Even so, there will be Mother and Father and friends to witness your merriment, heed your laughter and recognize your friendliness and love. By the time this letter winds its weary way across seas and lands to reach you, it will be the New Year.

So my Christmas love will be a belated love - yet love can never by belated since it is everlasting. In not too many days until your hands will touch mine in personal awareness - your breast will rest upon mine in peace - your lips will meet mine in promise - your eyes will exchange the tryst of our knowledge - you will be with me, and I and thee will be one as was meant to be before the scrolls of history and the screeds of mankind. Our trials and tribulations are not over. Indeed it is possible that your most severe tests lie ahead. There may be heartbreak and there may be heart-make. Which is to be will be by decree of the Great One, and it behooves us to be ready for the trumpet that gives us the chance to prove worthy of the trust in love.

I Love you,
LN

P.S. Always remember our 1942 Blue Buick and the happiness it brought us.

January 3, 1947

Keeper of Hearts,

Ah, my dear, there are so many things that I would write. I long to introduce you to this beautiful land. All would take mere words than grace the written language and more space that could brief a letter. Thus it is unwise to break the damn of my impatience. It is wise and best to await your actual presence. Then we can devote hours to reviewing our separate ways over the past four months and preparing ourselves for the work ahead. My arms are a tremble to know you again and my mind cannot accept as probable the imminence of your arrival. It required so many hours of careful preparation and endless hours of argument to clear the way for your heart's desire.

A few reservations persist in my mind but these, too, will wait your presence. Once I feel the unveiled intimacy of your lips, see the frank avowal of your eyes and hear the soft undertones of your voice - then I will know and believe that you rein Japan. In the meantime I can but pray the Great One to protect your world flight, comfort your mind and solace your heart, be of good cheer and of strong faith for the hope of the world and the hope of the heart are kindred in their precious dependence upon fortitude and courage despite the odds. Good night my Lady of Serene Silver - the morrow is coming.

I love you,
LN

April 8, 1949

Dear Deborah,

I have read the little note you enclosed "personal" regarding Col. Munton's view on your "love status". Giving advice on such a tender subject is very hard to do. One's own heart is really the only guide and I am sure when the time comes both of you will know.

I do agree that when talking about the future and career you should be more emphatic, and say that you look forward to gracing a home and being a devoted wife (to a man who gets very tired lately, as you have said).

The difference in age is something not to be dismissed. As well, of course, his wife and children need to be a part of the equation. No doubt you have both given this a great deal of thought.

My heart and love are with you always my dear daughter. I have to start dinner - you know Daddy and dinner.

I have enclosed a delicious recipe for an Easter Bunny Cake. I know you'll love it.

Love,
Mother

Ft. Bragg, NC. August 4, 1949

Dearly Beloved,

You are music in my heart. The wonder of your dearness is a constant thrill to me. One which neither familiarity nor intimacy can dull. There in is evidence of love as was meant in the beginning. Those lesser realities of living often create discord within intimacy - should one write, beclouding the perfect sky of romantic courting. Thrill is associated with rhythmic sound, pleasant sight, sweet taste and comforting feel and fragrant scent.

I went to the movies alone. Something I rarely do. The film was, "Too Late for Tears." The title made me think of you.

I love you,
LN

October 13, 1949

Ft. Bragg
Dearest Deborah,

I know how anxious you are to hear of the President's visit. It went off like a charm. The weather smiled on us all day. The schedule was carried out almost to the minute - which is no mean feat. The president seemed to enjoy himself- particularly at the luncheon. He had a horde of press reporters and photographers dogging his route. These were excluded from the visit to the Board - with no apparent repercussions to date.

At the luncheon the president permitted the press to join us at the conclusion when he made a few remarks. Two were pounced upon and made the headlines. One was his humorous reference to a loud speaker on the Board that could broadcast for two miles and a belief that it would have been a great aid to him on his touring of the country, which he didn't expect to do again. The press deduced that this meant, "Not run" for the next election when it is doubtful if the President was doing more than wisecracking.

191

A second reference to the battle, Air versus Navy, which the president concluded with a witty remark that after they had settled their differences the Army would step in and carry on as usual.

The local Munton-ites are in good fettle and anticipating the visit to D.C. in November. As yet the date is indeterminate. We must try and placate Carl's school schedule, my duty schedule and the desires to enjoy the trip. I will let you know as soon as the dates are set and you are "ordered" to reserve at least an evening for you and I. Carl is doing superior work in school and is beginning to become a member of the local "gang" of kids. He still anticipated DC and has a permanent warm spot in his heart for you. Often he recalls those card games with you with nostalgic comment. The neuritis that had Helen limping seems to be curing itself. We are hoping it was the result of some unnoticed bump that gave a local stiffness and soreness. At any rate the medics were unable to discover any cause and their limited pill treatment seems to be doing the trick.

. My mother was delighted to hear from you and I trust you two will mutually enjoy each other. My mother has lived an unusual life and I have, failed to date, to get her to record her adventures. She was a Yankee who married into the south at a time when feelings were high. She traveled most of her mature life, both theatrically and otherwise, to finally settle into the little mountain city she now adores. I too have been a nomad which makes me hesitant to declaim upon the settler versus nomad arguments that spring up at times.

Almost forgot, a letter from Lily indicates everything is okay. Her latest letter infers a better marital adjustment with hopes for a happy ending. Perhaps the addition of a child will do the trick. She had her last physical on the 11th, but I do not know the results. I have few fears for Lil has a rugged physical body - it is her temperament that might trip the issue.

Larry wants a boy and Lil is more or less adjusted to either. She mentioned receipt of your letter and admits some delay in answering which I know that you will understand. She promises to resume her correspondence once she is settled with the baby.

Few couples start their marriage with as much snarling troubles as did Larry and Lil. I have carefully refrained from participating in their life and will continue to do so until I am positive that they are adjusted.

Keep that little chin up high and do not falter in your new job. It takes courage, persistence and patience to end the game successfully. Some brilliant comets in life make grandiose effects and lash success as a heady diet. In the long run, the plugger who plans and persists comes out on top.

Adios for the time and remember that I am not only behind you in your effort for welfare and happiness but, with you.

The "Old" Boss

December 16, 1950

Beloved Woman,

This is the closing chapter of the 1950 record dedicated to the knowledge gained through the past twelve months, and to the faith in the ultimate wisdom of the next twelve months. If these words prove abstract it results from the obscurity of our times and uncertainty of our future.

History is a small voice whispering to all who listen, a warning on the rise and fall of mankind. Perchance this cycle has persisted even in civilizations lost behind the ice ages unto the very beginnings. Ignorance, distrust and doubt have dogged the lives of each person and thereby fostered the senses of self-importance, fear of inferiority and the challenge to competition.

As this oldest year ends, my twilight hope is that this Christmas will prove endearing and provide incentive for tomorrow. May you enjoy the period to the fullest. In the quiet moments remember the Master and his teachings, seek the calm inner peace of mind, and once or twice think of the man who loves you. With the break of the newest year, it is a time for reflection and determination. This is an ill time for jollity, indulgence and liberties. It is for dedication. With the dawn of Christ's day and the dusk of a lost year, my thoughts will be with you and join in a silent prayer that we may serve our times well and in the serving attain a better understanding of our times and ourselves. Life has given us wondrous opportunities and an immortal love. We should plan to give life our dedication and support that those who follow may know opportunity without fear.

I love you,
Forever LN

April 8, 1950

Adorable Woman,

Your lilting voice last Friday was a breath of spring and the essence of love. I was at a disadvantage. Five solemn faced officers ringed me, and Rosemary sat beside me. We were completing a conference. Hence my controlled "front". How did I do? Instinct had me clear Rosemary from the line before you answered. As a rule Rosemary takes the call and then records the conversation. This must be remembered. As I took over and heard the unusual interference a flash told me that you were calling. I told Rosemary to hang up to improve the line and I would call her in if this were necessary. My heart felt the beat of your love and your words assured me that each meant I love you. Bless your lovely heart; it was so very good to hear the ring of happiness and the touch of a trip well done.

A silent whisper entered my thoughts the other night. It warned that great happiness, or great sorrow, lay beyond knowledge of you.

A pause descended upon the real "me" as the question arose - to seek peace of inaction or chance serenity through daring. I chose to dare and did my best to tell you of the gauntlet - so that you would not accept the dare through thoughtlessness or ignorance of the powers invested herein. The Tale is yet to be told. The pages turn slowly and each brings its incidents, its tensions, its peace and its knowledge. Even the number of chapters may only be guessed. Someday the Book will attain "Finis". With sincerity and faith - I pray that this Finis will be beyond time and question amid the certainty of all tomorrows wrapped into one.

April is noted for radiance over another day. Can you guess? This is my heart's knowledge and to be divulged only when your eyes may confess to mine and your lips may smile with mine to the inner assurance like no other peace on earth.

Mine heart - I see no reason why you should not wire Del Haven Md for a cabin on Friday night the 14th, and plan to leave your car at the Capitol Saturday. You can lock your valuables in the rear of the car and leave large items in the back seat. Take your keys to the car and leave the ignition on. I doubt if there is real risk to lose. I plan to drive to Roanoke during the night of the 14th and meet you on the evening train Saturday the 15th. I will leave this in your capable hands. I expect a letter from you by Wednesday, but try to avoid mailing anything after Tuesday. If need be, wire me at 1138 2nd St. and sign same "Nelson" with any change or trouble. My heart aches to be with you. Soon my dear, soon.

Love my dear,
LN

January 5, 1962

Dear Deborah,

As you know, the hour has fallen. Col. Munton's death came on the evening of December 21. It was so near to the Christmas season that I planned to write to you later. However, I talked to Maureen a few days afterward and she told me that someone had already informed you.

Carl was already on the West Coast when the news came. I'll never forget how helpful the Red Cross people were. They finally reached Carl two hours before his flight to Okinawa. Talk about providential! He finally arrived home on the 21st. It was next to impossible to get a flight to New York, then flew down to Friendship from there.

Lily also had a rough time reaching here, owing to the holiday season travel.

Col. Munton had a beautiful and impressive service. Quite a few came to the Fort Myer Chapel and more came to the graveside. He is buried in a beautiful part of the cemetery overlooking the Potomac, much like his hero George Washington.

As you can well imagine, there is a mountain of mail to answer. Some letters are still arriving. Today I received a heartwarming note from your dad.

I'm sure that you have some questions. If so, ask me in your next letter.

Now I want to thank you for the lovely billfold. The design is beautiful; I plan to use it in my navy blue handbag. It was such a queer Christmas. Cards were arriving in the same mail with sympathy notes. Lily had to leave on the 23rd to be with her family and plan their Christmas.

It is also very important to me to thank you for the years of dedicated service you showed to my husband and our family. So often the Colonel would mention how lost he would have been without you. I know the sacrifices you have made, and I want you to know how much I appreciate your unwavering loyalty to the Colonel and me.

I am doing well. Carl was simply wonderful. I had put a small frosty pink tree in the dining room window before the sad news came. We left it there and on Christmas morning there were gaily wrapped packages around it even though Carl and I had exchanged gifts before he left the first time. I hope you received the two items I sent. The clerk who waited on me had never heard of SHAPE so she wrote Shape on the address. I corrected her, but she didn't seem very sharp.

Well I have some other chores to do, so will sign off now.

I hope your New Year will be a wonderful one.

Affectionately,
Helen Munton

Epilogue:

I found it so sad and rather curious to see the rest of the pages in Deborah's journal left blank after her last entry on Tuesday, August 14, 1945. It was as though Deborah knew that that chapter of her life had ended and a new one was beginning.

After having read her journals, and having such intimate knowledge of Deborah's life, I felt I needed to find out what became of the people who meant so much to her during her cherry blossom years.

My mother-in-law's sister Carol, who had visited Deborah in Washington, and who was so close to her growing up, had married and had three lovely daughters. Col. Munton and Deborah were in fact Carol's oldest daughter, Judy's, Godparents. I decided to call Judy and asked if we could meet. I was hoping she could help to fill in some of the missing pages.

Judy joined me for dinner at the Saturn Club on a lovely warm evening in April. We sat out on the courtyard, much like Deborah and her parents had years ago with their friends. It was ironically the beginning of cherry blossom season in Buffalo, and there were small bowls of soft pink blossoms on each table with tea lights surrounding them. I had ordered two Daiquiri's for us in honor of Deborah.

Judy had known about Deborah and the colonel's relationship for years. Carol had confided in her daughter after Judy had asked some probing questions. I was thankful and content with what Judy had to share with me.

On the occasion of Col. Munton's 50th birthday, the colonel and Deborah had been walking the streets of Paris when they came upon an artist painting a scene with their apartment in the distance, and the steeple of a church with vines of roses climbing along the stone walls. He offered to buy it for her, but she refused. She wanted to buy the painting for him to take home. She felt that it could be their secret, and no one would realize the significance that it held.

From what Judy told me it appeared that their relationship during the 1950's was less defined. It seemed that as Deborah's career began to take off she became more confident and independent. She was creating that next chapter of her life, and she was doing it on her own.

At the age of 61, the colonel was succumbing to the ravages of Lou Gehrig's disease, which he had been battling for several years. When Deborah visited him in the Catholic Hospital where Mrs. Munton had placed him, a nun approached her before she entered his room, as she had not met Deborah before she wanted to prepare her for his condition. He was in the end stages of his illness and was suffering from mild dementia. She wanted Deborah to be aware that he may or may not know her.

Deborah had been extremely busy and traveling a great deal with her new position. She had tried to make time to visit him, but work and other commitments kept getting in the way. She was shocked and saddened by his appearance; no longer the strong and vital man she had once known. Those deep blue eyes were staring at her and she knew that he was clear of mind, at least for that moment.

Deborah stood beside his bed and took his cold, frail hand in hers. She did not kiss him, but warmed his hand gently in hers. His wedding ring slipped from his finger and fell to the floor, spinning across the room. She bent down to pick it up, and as she stood she found herself standing in front of a stirring painting of the Madonna and Child at the foot of his bed. How many times had she thought of having a child, being a mother, a wife?

Sister came in to see if she had any questions and noticed her standing, staring at the painting, rooted in place, almost unable to move. She quietly stood by Deborah's side and explained how the painting had greatly agitated the colonel when he was first admitted. He said that the painting was judging him. She had offered to remove it, but Helen and Lily merely felt it was his illness speaking and told her to leave it as it was.

Deborah thanked the sister, and went to his bedside slipping the ring back on to his finger. She knew there was one last gesture she could make to comfort her Lord Nelson. She drove to his home and after sharing a cup of tea and news of the family with Helen, asked if she could go into the colonel's study. There she knew she would find the painting from Paris. It was hanging on the opposite wall from his desk in a position for him to look at every day. She asked if she might take it to his hospital room, with the thought that something familiar from home might comfort him. Helen said she doubted that he would remember the painting, but thought that it was a kind gesture on Deborah's part.

Deborah drove back to his hospital room, and with the sister's permission, took down the painting of Mary and Jesus, and hung the colorful, street market scene, with the bit of their apartment top, church steeple and out of place Cherry Blossoms.

And Jake? I did ask my mother-in-law what became of him and she shared a conversation she had had with Deborah many years after the war. They were sitting in lounge chairs in the sand at Crystal Beach watching the kids filling their sand pails and chasing waves as they rolled up after their little feet. Laura said that she casually asked Deborah whatever happened to that sweet boy who was so in love with her during the war?

Deborah paused as she lit another cigarette, and with very little reflection or emotion bluntly stated, "He walked into the Gulf of Mexico. His sister called me. It was when I moved to Japan."

Yet Jake must have meant something to Deborah. Perhaps it was easier to dismiss than to live with.

I found a newspaper clipping in Deborah's memory box. It must have been from one of the war magazines that were published in Washington at that time. It was dated Jan. 12, 1943.

"Corporal Jake O'Malley has been assigned to army recruiting headquarters in the Federal building to interview prospective members of the Women's Army Corps who also are interested in entering the Air Transport Command.

His service record reads like a combination of the travels of Marco Polo and a thrill-packed Western novel.

He entered the army June 5, 1942, and after training at Fort Bragg, North Carolina, was transferred to India to begin operation of an office for the China-Burma-India wing of the Air Transport Command. Besides the 20 round-trip hops over the Himalayas, Corporal O'Malley also found time to do a little of what he describes as "food-dropping duty." This consisted of flying over secret allied weather stations in the Himalaya foothills and dropping food parcels by parachute.

But the high-light of his over-seas career came the day when two Jap Zeros attacked the transport plane in which he was riding high above the Negia foothills which are adjacent to the Himalayas. Corporal O'Malley recalls that his crew ducked the big allied transport plane into the foothills, radioed for help and "sweat it out" for 30 minutes before aid arrived.

"Some P-38's came to our rescue just in time, because we had fooled the Zeros with low-altitude flying long enough," he declared.

After that venture, he underwent many more before suffering a partial paralysis of both legs which forced him to return to the United States.

After visiting several army hospitals Corporal O'Malley declared: "I'm really enthusiastic about WAC recruiting because I know what valuable service members of the Women's Army Corps can give in the Air Transport Command. Women have been a very important part of winning this war - I've seen them in action."

Finis

* * *

One last note: As I was placing all of Deborah's memories back in the blue satin box, a black and white postcard fell out of her copy of "Rebecca." It was a post card in black and white of the Napoli Via Carocciola - Hotel Royal. On the front there was written "Our Room" #851, with a postmark August 1963. When I turned it over it read, "Dear Deborah, Room 851 isn't the same without you. Are you coming to Naples next month? I will be here. Love, Ricardo."

Bravo! Deborah! Bravo!

He has not really tasted life
Who does not know the earthly things?
The misty beauty of a pale sunrise,
The soothing rain, the wind that sighs,
The ocean's booming, overwhelming swell,
That grips the soul with awesome spell,
The perfume of the burning leaves,
That fills the magical October eves,
The stars that flood the blue at night,
And trees aglow with bright moonlight.
He has not really tasted life
Who has not seen and felt these things:
The haunting mystery at Christmas time,
The burning candles, bells that chime,
Pink glasses, shining silverware,

And children's voice in the air,

A heart that knows a rapid beat,

When bands keep step with marching feet,

The songs that praise your native land,

The flag that symbolized freedom's hand.

He has not really tasted life

Who does not know emotion's fire?

The love that tear-dimmed eyes convey,

The peace that loving arms portray,

A soul that soars as if on wings,

With the yearning that Ambition brings,

The pain, the joy, and endless strife,

These are the essence of human life:

If you have met with all these things,

Your wealth surpasses that of Kings.

Deborah Peters

Armistice Day - November 11, 1938

Mary Mullett-Flynn

is a writer and watercolor artist in Buffalo New York and owns a small shop, Back of the Moon: Gifts & Gallery, showcasing her moon inspired paintings and whimsical gifts located in Wilson, York. She has conducted writing workshops at the Chautauqua Institute , Just Buffalo Literary Center, and The Albright Knox Art Gallery working with children through their, A Picture's Worth a Thousand Words program, pairing docents with writers. She lives in Kenmore, New York with her husband Patrick, son, Evan and puppy Lily.

**Look for Pre-quel Deborah's Diaries The Buffalo Years –
1937 - 1940**

Coming in Spring 2016

Deborah's Diaries The Buffalo Years – 1937 - 1940 introduces
Deborah as a seventeen year old girl, learning to speak French,
heading to the theater to see Gone With the Wind over and over,
hitting all the hot spots of Buffalo's night life including Laubes Old
Spain Restaurant, The Wishing Well Tavern, with an authentic 125
year old Wishing Well, The Statler, McVan's Night Club, Peter A
Weil's Tavern, The Peter Stuyvesant Room, with their glass dance
floor, and so much more.

She takes us on a tour of Buffalo back to a time few can remember,
but all will never forget.

Sequel

Made in the USA
Middletown, DE
27 May 2015